"Dr. Richard Land is an articulate voice with intellectual depth who has been an effective spokesman for the cause of Christ in the public square."

Dr. James C. Dobson
Founder and Chairman, Focus on the Family

"Richard Land brings clear thinking and an astute voice to the ethics debate in America today. He expresses the case for religious liberty in a way that is both thought-provoking and convincing. Dr. Land is a man of faith, whose personal commitment to his public views is refreshing and highly compelling."

William J. Bennett
Secretary of Education during the Reagan Administration and Director of the Office of National Drug Control Policy under former President Bush

"Richard is a gifted leader who well understands the cultural crisis of our age and eloquently addresses the solution."

Charles Colson
Founder, Prison Fellowship Ministries

"Richard Land has led Southern Baptists with clarity, conviction, and compassion. His mind is keen, his heart is warm, and his courage is dauntless."

Dr. Adrian P. Rogers
Retired Pastor, Bellevue Baptist Church
Memphis, Tennessee

"Once in a great while there is born into God's world a character at once so colorful, so unique, so perceptive, and so incisive that whether you love him or despise him, you cannot ignore him. If ever a contemporary figure fit that mold, Richard Land, scholar, theologian, historian, pastor, is that man."

Dr. Paige Patterson
President, Southwestern Baptist Theological Seminary

IMAGINE! A GOD-BLESSED AMERICA

IMAGINE! A GOD-BLESSED AMERICA

How It *Could* Happen
and What It Would Look Like

RICHARD LAND

BROADMAN
&HOLMAN
PUBLISHERS

NASHVILLE, TENNESSEE

Ten-Digit ISBN: 0–8054–2765–1
Thirteen-Digit ISBN: 978-0–8054–2765–3

Published by Broadman & Holman Publishers
Nashville, Tennessee

Dewey Decimal Classification: 170
Subject Heading: AMERICAN ETHICS \ AMERICAN-
RELIGIOUS LIFE \ UNITED STATES-MORAL CONDITIONS

1 2 3 4 5 6 7 8 9 10 09 08 07 06 05

To Jennifer, Richard Jr., and Rachel,
through whom I experienced the wonder of fatherhood,
and who are my personal links to America's future.

CONTENTS

PREFACE

A s this book is being prepared for publication, sixties icon Bob
Dylan is showing up on the bestseller lists with the first volume of his memoirs. The times, they are a-changin.'

"God bless America" rang in the ears of my parents' generation
as singer Kate Smith belted her way into America's homes through
the scratchy reception of the family radio. First performed on
Armistice Day, 1938—observing the twenty-year anniversary of
the end of World War I—the song became a fervent prayer for a
nation recovering from one global conflict and soon to be engulfed
in another.

For my generation, raised on television images of a war that
divided the country and a civil rights struggle rooted in our worst
national anguish a century earlier, the lyrics of Irving Berlin gave
way to those of John Lennon. A countercurrent of social protest
flushed the national pride of "God bless America" down the gutter
of antinationalism with song lyrics inviting us to "imagine . . .
there's no country."

My children have come of age in a generation scarred by a
nightmare vision of America's literal undoing in the catastrophic

events of September 11, 2001. "God bless America" has again become a rallying cry, echoing in civil gatherings from the Capitol steps to the seventh-inning stretch of major-league baseball games. But sixty-three years later, what do these words mean for a country that has spent decades deconstructing its national affirmations about belief in God's sovereignty?

When a reporter asked me, "What do you mean when you say 'God bless America,'" I couldn't stop thinking about an answer. Does America deserve to be blessed? Is God on "our side"? What would such blessing look like, if God chose to grant it?

My initial answer to this question became a book based on God's conditional promise in 2 Chronicles 7:14. *Real Homeland Security* explored what would need to happen in order for God to bless America—beginning with the heart of each believer and extending to a possible revival and reformation across our land.

Even after completing that book, I found that I couldn't stop thinking about the America God might bless. What if the number of Christians who dedicated themselves to living out God's call to repentance and obedience so increased that it reached a divine tipping point of God's blessing? How would our country be changed by the pouring out of God's healing upon our land? What would it really look like?

I also wondered why more Christians were not asking these kinds of questions—except to point out why God would not bless America in her current condition. Why did John Lennon's false vision have such staying power, and where were the Christian visions that could offer a radical, positive alternative to the cries and whispers of a decaying culture? Had we retreated to a doom-and-gloom corner of end-times fixation? Were we giving up on the possibility that there might yet be another great revival and reformation among God's people before the second coming of our Lord?

"You may say I'm a dreamer," crooned John Lennon, "but I'm not the only one." Here is what I would like to say to you through this book: Let us refuse to leave the future of this country to those who dream impossible dreams of man-made utopias. Let us refuse to settle for merely "Christian" dreams, which never rise above wishful thinking, while we wring our hands and tsk our tongues over how much worse things will get before Christ returns. Let us commit ourselves to a vision of humbling ourselves, praying, seeking God's face, and turning from our wicked ways . . . a vision of what our country might become if the blessing of God Almighty began to turn the tide.

And so I invite you to imagine with me—prayerfully, and in your own private place of meeting with the Lord Jesus Christ—a God-blessed America. . . .

ACKNOWLEDGMENTS

I am grateful for the contributions of my many friends and colleagues who shared in the creation of this project. It was truly a team effort, and I am sincerely grateful to all who served in this task, especially my writing partner, Kathy Helmers, who quickly captured the vision for this project. Her research, deciphering of my disgraphic scribblings, and phone interviews were invaluable. This project never would have happened without Kathy's help.

I also would like to express my deepest appreciation to my family. I am grateful to my wife Becky, who has been my ministry partner for more than thirty-four years. I couldn't do what I do without her love and self-sacrificial support. My three children not only bring me profound joy, but also have played an important part in my ministry. Jennifer, Richard Jr., and Rachel—you are so indescribably precious to me! My two proudest titles are husband and dad.

I also would like to express my gratitude to my diligent staff, who labor above and beyond the call of duty. God has given me an incredible ministry team of which I am very appreciative. Their commitment, skill, encouragement, and servant hearts have been a deep inspiration to me. Thanks go to Kerry Bural, Doug Carlton, Amber Chesser, Pat Clark, Karen Cole, Barrett Duke, Jacob Fentress, Harold Harper, Dwayne Hastings, Matt Hawkins, Barbara Jester, Lana Kimbro, Judy Lawson, Jerry Price, Bobby Reed, Tom Strode, Brian Terrell, and Sulyn Wilkins.

Thanks also to all of my colaborers and partners in the harvest who listen to our radio programs, *For Faith & Family* and *Richard Land LIVE!* who pray for our ministry, and who support us financially. Your prayers and letters of encouragement mean a great deal to our staff and to me personally.

Most of all, I am grateful for my Heavenly Father and God's Son, my Savior, the coming King, Jesus the Christ. May He use this book for His kingdom and His glory, and may He continue to bless the United States of America.

· 1 ·

Could the Best Be Yet to Be?

IMAGINE! AN AMERICA
BLESSED BY GOD

Have you ever imagined what life would be like if all your hopes and prayers came true? Think about what you have prayed for in the last six months. Now visualize life with positive answers to those prayers. What does it look like?

Perhaps your relationship with the Lord is more vibrant . . . you are experiencing conviction of sin, confessing your sin, and tasting the freedom of forgiveness . . . your relationship with your spouse is blossoming in a renewed way, and together you are anticipating the leading of the Lord for this season of your lives . . . parents and siblings in your family have overcome bitterness and distance and are living in harmony . . . an illness is healed, or a

1

financial crisis resolved . . . the scars of a broken relationship or the wounds of past mistakes are mended . . . your church community or small group provides the safety and support you need . . . the neighborhood is improving . . . your candidate of choice gets elected to public office . . . global conflicts yield peace initiatives instead of worsening violence.

Suppose we imagined what our country would look like if we prayed "God bless America"—and then God answered by pouring out blessings upon us? I don't mean what would happen if evangelicals scored a few victories in the political arena. I'm talking about a wholesale revival sweeping through our land: families, neighborhoods, social institutions, churches, government, and corporations. What would a *divinely healed* America look like?

THE POWER OF DREAMS

Over thirty years ago, John Lennon conjured up a vision of what the world would look like if his own dreams came true. His song "Imagine,"[1] which describes a peace-and-love utopia of secular humanism and global harmony, has become an anthem of pop-culture pipe dreams for succeeding generations. Lennon dreamed of a world for which there was no cause worth dying, no God, no religion, and no heaven or hell. How much more secular and hostile to religion can you be?

Lennon's widow, Yoko Ono, continues to carry the peace-making banner she and her husband championed in the 1960s. In an interview with Amnesty International, an organization partnering with her for their *Imagine* campaign, she commented, "We are all dreamers creating the next world, the next beautiful world for ourselves and for our children."[2] Notice the connection from *dreaming* to *creating the next world*. Yoko Ono has been working hard to make the "Imagine" daydreams come true. Even a false vision can inspire action.

What daydreams are Christians conjuring in our day? Whose dreams are we helping to make come true?

Fidel Castro, the communist dictator of Cuba who took power in the 1959 revolution, initially condemned the Beatles' music as a decadent Western influence. But on the twentieth anniversary of Lennon's death, he commissioned a public sculpture of the pop star sitting on a Havana bench. The lyrics of "Imagine" suited his idea of the perfect society. "What makes him great in my eyes is his thinking, his ideas," Castro announced. "I share his dreams completely. I too am a dreamer who has seen his dreams turn into reality."[3] Oh really? Did we all miss something, or have heaven and hell outlasted John Lennon's dreams of their disappearance?

A dream is a wish that something would come true; a vision is just a vivid dream unless it is accompanied by a commitment to make it happen. Castro turned his dreams into a vision—and that nightmare vision has become reality for an entire nation locked in his grip for nearly five decades.

Whose vision of America are we living with today? Do Christians have a truly biblical vision for our country? Are we committing ourselves to making it become a reality?

HAVE WE FORGOTTEN HOW TO DREAM?

Millions of Christians affirm a form of political activism, and rightly so. But it tilts toward an imbalanced form of activism when it addresses only a litmus-test list of issues without an undergirding foundation: a balanced understanding of the three ordained institutions enabling us to fulfill our God-given purposes—family, church, and civil government.

An "issues-only" focus narrows our sight to temporal political agendas. A truly biblical vision opens our sight to the transforming power of the gospel in *all* of life. We lose sight of the forest when we're squinting hard at the trees—but we forget that there are entirely different kinds of forests that God graciously brings to life.

Why have we too often abdicated the role of visionaries for our culture, surrendering it to those who would take us further into moral and spiritual decline?

Others retreat from the public policy arena, convinced that we're living in the end times. Since the world is spiraling downward into global conflicts and natural disasters, they reason, why spend energy on social change? They reject political involvement for personal evangelism, presuming that the Rapture is imminent.

Although my own views on eschatology align with a pre-tribulation rapture of believers, I believe that there could be yet another Great Awakening in our country, a nationwide revival. Indeed, I believe that spiritual revival could ripen into another Reformation that would shake America for Christ as significantly as Luther and Calvin shook Europe, and Whitfield, Wesley, and Edwards shook Great Britain and colonial America, before the spiritual and moral decline that portends Christ's second coming engulfs civilization.

Scripture tells us that none of us can know with certainty the day or hour of the Lord's return. Thus, we have no right to abandon the world to its own misery. Nowhere in Scripture are we called to huddle pessimistically in Christian ghettos, snatching converts out of the world. In fact, we're commanded to do quite the opposite: to live fully in the world but not of it, making the most of the time we do have, because *none of us knows* when the Lord's return will occur. What we do know is that we're supposed to believe and practice what the Bible teaches.

The Bible teaches that I am to trust my life to the Lord; He comes and lives in my life and changes me so I am born again from above; and I am to live a life committed to His teachings—and He gives me the power to do that. I'm not responsible for the timetable of the eschatological future. Just because I have an eschatological view that is premillennial does not preclude the fact that there could be a glorious revival and Reformation. But if we don't envision it, it won't happen. And it won't happen unless individual people of faith commit themselves to living godly lives.

Have we become so consumed with speculation about the end that we have forgotten how to dream of, or even imagine, the possibility of another Reformation?

A DIVINE VISION FOR AMERICA

In March 2000, the ninety-sixth American Assembly entitled "Religion in Public Life" gathered fifty-seven men and women from government, business, labor, law, academia, nonprofit organizations, the media, different religious faiths, and faith-based organizations to define policies and actions about the role of religion in American public life. Their recommendations affirmed a deep commitment to the importance of vigorous religious involvement in public policy and civic life:

> Americans should recognize that they live in a country with strong and flexible institutions, and a remarkable capacity for living with—and sometimes resolving—intensely conflicting views without recourse to violence. Religious voices are a vital component of our national conversation, and should be heard in the public square. We reject the notion that religion is exclusively a private matter relegated to the homes and sacred meeting places of the faithful, primarily for two reasons. First, religious convictions of individuals cannot be severed from their daily lives. People of faith in business, law, medicine, education, and other sectors should not be required to divorce their faith from their professions. Second, many religious communities have a rich tradition of constructive social engagement and our nation benefits from their work in such varied areas as social justice, civil rights, and ethics. We encourage people of faith to foster the emergence of a new American generation, one that better comprehends the significance of the increasing religious pluralism in this nation, and its implications for advancing civic dialogue.[4]

Where are the voices from our evangelical communities seeking to advance understanding of, and appreciation for, the contributions that Christians can make to our nation's public life, to the benefit of all citizens? According to some statistics, 40 percent of Christians in America consider themselves "born again." Only 14 percent are actually living it out on any kind of daily basis.

In 2 Chronicles 7:14, we have God's promise that if enough of His people humble themselves, seek His face, pray, and turn from their wicked ways, He will forgive their sin and heal their land. As I described in *Real Homeland Security*,[5] this passage gives us a divine picture of the America that God will bless. It is a picture of people repenting—not unbelievers, but believers—with a heart-piercing conviction of how far short they have fallen from God's desire for His people.

We need a bracing, compelling vision of what this outpouring of blessing could look like. One thing it would *not* be—going back to "the good old days" before the 1960s came along and secularized and paganized our culture. Life in 1950s postwar America may have been great for *some* people, but not for those oppressed by the institutional evil of racism and/or by the refusal to grant women their constitutional rights to equal treatment under the law.

No, I am not advocating a return to some glorious past. I want us to go forward to a future we have never seen.

It doesn't mean trying to impose Christianity on our society by government edict. God forbid that we should, and would, impose a theocracy. The legitimate separation of church and state is a principle that protects both institutions.

I am not calling for an officially "Christian America." I want us to envision a country in which most of its citizens are Christians, or are living according to the core values of a Judeo-Christian worldview, and thus, the nation's culture and society reflect Judeo-Christian values.

Whose dreams are becoming the visions that shape our future as a nation? This is serious business. When God's people shrink back from a bold, biblical vision for the community, the city, the country in which they live, walling themselves off to meet their own needs and neglecting to take the gospel out into society in speech and in action as salt and light, the church becomes afflicted with "ingrown eyeballs."

Sports research has demonstrated that if you can visualize a better performance, you can improve your performance. Imagining a better golf swing can actually make you a better golfer. From discoveries in neuroscience, we know why this is so: the brain circuits involved in visualizing something are the same circuits involved in processing information we acquire through our visual sense. The brain can maintain records of what it "sees" in these circuits, without distinguishing whether that information came from without, through external sources, or from within, through the brain's power of imagination.

Ken Paller and Brian Gonsalves of Northwestern University conducted a study in which they were able to induce subjects to remember something that had never happened.[6] This is why it is so controversial to attempt to reconstruct past events based only on a person's memory: memories can be "created" through the power of suggestion.

The flip side of this potentially negative phenomenon is the power of visualizing—what Andy Stanley has described as "visioneering"—to bring about powerful and positive change, starting only with the conviction that change needs to happen.

Vision often begins with the inability to accept things the way they are. Over time that dissatisfaction matures into a clear picture of what could be. But a vision is more than that. After all, what could be is an idea, a dream, but not necessarily a vision.

There is always a moral element to vision. Vision carries with it a sense of conviction. Anyone with a vision will tell you this is not merely something that could be done. This is something that should be done. This is something that must happen. It is this element that catapults men and women out of the realm of passive concern and into action. It is the moral element that gives a vision a sense of urgency.

Vision is a clear mental picture of what could be, fueled by the conviction that it should be.[7]

Christians are often accused of being known more for what they are against than what they are for—and there are a lot of false visions circulating throughout our culture. Who is offering authentic ones?

During the civil rights movement, Robert Kennedy paraphrased George Bernard Shaw when he so famously stated, "Some people see things the way they are and ask, 'Why?' I dream of things that never were and ask, 'Why not?'"

In this book, I want us to imagine together what it would look like if we were to see God truly bless America as He has promised He will do under the conditions He has laid down. Why *not* revival in America, why *not* Reformation, and why *not* in our time?

LET'S IMAGINE A FUTURE FOR AMERICA

If John Lennon's dream of a godless, secular-humanist world were to come true, think of what it might look like:

- A neopaganist triumph ushering in a widespread decline on the issues that matter most.

- Human life would become much more commoditized. Clone plantations would produce Frankensteinian tragedies. Women would sell their eggs in the name of producing engineered children. There would be abundant harvests of fetal tissue to prolong the lives of narcissistic people.

- Children would be vulnerable to the sexual appetites of adults. The pedophile movement would have achieved the social acceptance accorded the homosexual movement currently. The age of consent would be lowered, and children would be sexualized at earlier and earlier ages. The sexual abuse and molestation of children would multiply exponentially.

- Pornography would be at epidemic proportions. Hard-core porn would be regular fare on television.

- Religious freedom would be snuffed out. Neopagan orthodoxy would be extremely intolerant of any opponent. Those who hold to a Judeo-Christian worldview would find themselves vilified at best and legally restricted at worst for opposing neopagan ideology. The *one* thing abject moral relativists cannot tolerate is people who believe in moral absolutes.

Even a false vision has great power. Imagine what a true vision of biblical transformation could bring to life:

- In your city, the last rape occurred three years ago.
- The local prison has been converted to a museum because there are so few prisoners to house.
- Women and children can walk the streets without fear of physical or sexual assault.
- Students can walk the hallways of public schools with little, if any, thought for their physical safety.
- Four out of five nursing homes have closed down, because our culture values the aging and families are committed to all their members.
- Most children know their grandparents and extended family members because they live near them or visit them regularly.
- There are no air quality alerts because we are good stewards of the environment and therefore people are breathing clean air.
- No one can remember the last time there was a need for shelters to protect victims of domestic abuse.
- There aren't any rescue organizations for abused and abandoned animals, because we treat animals with respect.

Is this a dream? Just hopeless pie-in-the-sky, heaven-on-earth nonsense, a Christian version of a fantasy utopia? Well, *someone's* vision is going to prevail, and the future will be shaped by it. Whose will it be?

I want to set forth a challenge to all of us: let us turn our hearts to the Lord and pray, in the spirit of the prophet Habakkuk, "Lord, we have heard of your fame; we stand in awe of your mighty deeds among your people, O Lord. Renew them in our day, in our time make them known."[8] And then let us cast our eyes toward a vision of what we yearn and hunger for our country's future to be: a God-blessed America.

God has worked such miracles before. God *is* working miracles every minute of every hour of every day. Let it begin with us. Let it begin now.

· 2 ·

Why your faith matters so much . . .

IT CAN HAPPEN HERE

In the late eighteenth century, as England nursed the wounds of losing the war with the colonists in America, its ruling classes descended further into a culture of decadence. Political corruption was rampant as poverty devastated the masses. The horrors of child labor spawned by the budding industrial revolution were in full swing. City life was dirty and dangerous, rife with crime, unchecked cruelty to animals, and appalling prison conditions. On top of all this, the economy was driven in large part by the monstrous evils of the slave trade.

Against this tide of wickedness stood a little man barely five feet tall, afflicted with chronic health problems. His privileged background had ushered him through the finest education available and into early political success, and he enjoyed all the worldly pleasures of the privileged classes. Then he had an encounter with Christ, changing him from the inside out, and he considered abandoning his successful career to throw himself into ministry. His close friend John Newton, the reformed slave-ship captain who composed the hymn "Amazing Grace," convinced him that he could serve Christ best by remaining in the public arena to champion righteousness against the evils of the day.

William Wilberforce was this mouse who roared—eloquently; he was a brilliant orator. With the support of his small band of fellow Christians (the "Clapham sect"), he persevered in loving and obeying the gospel of Christ in reform efforts for nearly five decades before succumbing to illness at age seventy-four. His life goal was twofold: to work for an end to the slave trade and to help reform the moral character of Britain. Wilberforce's astonishing record of social change included an end to the slave trade after twenty years of struggle, followed by twenty-six years of further struggle to abolish slavery in England altogether.

Throughout his campaign, Wilberforce was on the one side attacked verbally and physically by supporters of the slave trade who abhorred his efforts to end their lucrative business, and on the other side he was often vilified by Christian abolitionists who accused him of moving too slowly and compromising with the enemy. Yet he never lost sight of the fact that political strategies and legal reforms were eclipsed by the more fundamental need of his country for citizens who persevered, loving and obeying Jesus in the midst of a mocking and degenerate age to love and obey the gospel.

ANOTHER UNLIKELY HERO

If a journey of a thousand miles begins with a single step, then the spiritual transformation of an entire nation begins with the spiritual transformation of a single life. Could it be yours? *Should* it be yours?

Another lone figure called upon to stand against the national crisis of his day was the flawed and reluctant leader Gideon. When an angel of the Lord appeared to commission him to lead Israel against their oppressors, the angel hailed Gideon by saying, "The LORD is with you, mighty warrior."[9] Gideon did not exactly respond in kind. He replied by questioning whether or not the Lord really *was* with him and His people. Where were all those Red Sea wonders now that the Israelites were terribly oppressed by the Midianites, seemingly abandoned by God?

Well, said the Lord through His messenger, "Go in the strength you have and save Israel out of Midian's hand. Am I not sending you?" (Judges 6:14). This wasn't enough to bolster Gideon's confidence, either. Gideon protested that his clan was the weakest in the tribe of Manasseh—and that Gideon was the weakest member of his family.

The Lord answered Gideon's pathetic complaints and protests with the assurance of His presence and power: "I will be with you, and you will strike down all the Midianites together" (Judges 6:16).

You can almost see Gideon wringing his hands as he told God "Okay, if you really are going to be with me in this, how about a sign so that I know it's really *you* talking? Could you wait a minute while I run and get an offering to put in front of you?"

Isn't God amazing? All He said in reply to this protracted resistance was, "I will wait until you return."

Gideon got the assurance he was looking for, but it didn't keep him from asking for a sign yet again when fear got the better of him. And again, God patiently answered with assurance. However, before his mission was accomplished, Gideon would learn without a doubt that the only reason he could succeed was through the power of God.

When the time arrived for battle, Gideon started the day with thirty-two thousand men. By nighttime, as the enemy camps settled in the valley "thick as locusts" (Judges 7:12), with so many camels they could no more be counted than grains of sand on the seashore, God had instructed Gideon to whittle down his troops to just three hundred men.

The rest is history—fascinating and instructive history, in which one unlikely leader obeyed the Lord's commands and conquered a vast nation with a hardy little band of brothers. God will meet us where we are, make us what He wants us to be, and take us where He wants us to go, if we will only surrender to His will and allow Him to work *His* purpose in our lives.

What Will It Take for Change to Occur?

In July 2004, thousands of people descended upon Barcelona, Spain, to convene the fourth-ever Council for a Parliament of the World's Religions. The council, inaugurated in 1893 at a gathering in Chicago of Jews, Catholics, Bahais, Hindus, and Buddhists, was revived a second time one hundred years later in Chicago with a centennial observance attended by eight thousand people from diverse traditions and regions of the world. The third meeting of the council took place in 1999 in Cape Town, South Africa, to affirm the role of spiritual communities in the struggle against apartheid and in confronting the rising AIDS epidemic.

The primary purpose of the Parliament of the World's Religions is to seek pathways to peace through harmonious cooperation among diverse religious groups. In 2004, the council partnered with the Universal Forum of Cultures, a coalition sponsoring a five-month-long event involving *millions* of people in dialogue to promote international peace and cooperation.

There have been no announcements about whether this massive endeavor is having ripple effects in positive results. If size alone mattered, we would be seeing wondrous changes indeed. Sadly, however, these well-intentioned gatherings seem to have faded with the brief news headlines they made, if visible results are any measure of their success in bringing peace to our conflict-ridden world.

How ironic that in the annals of history, the name of one little man in England who managed to alienate both sides of the controversy of his day would be memorialized as a champion of social reform and role model of faith, while millions of people attending one of the world's biggest religious events would remain nameless, simply disappearing into the statistical records of an organization that seems to have little more to show for its efforts than the statistics of its gatherings.

What will it take for spiritual awakening to engulf our nation? What are the conditions under which God will bless America?

STANDING ON THE PROMISE

We know from the Scriptures that it doesn't take millions of people cooperating with one another to bring about social change:

"If my people, who are called by my name . . ."—the most important agents of change are *believers;*

". . . will humble themselves and pray and seek my face and turn from their wicked ways . . ."—not gather in great numbers to talk about change, but get down on their knees to change their hearts before God;

". . . then I will hear from heaven and forgive their sin and will heal their land"—and blessings will pour out on just and unjust alike.

Place this promise next to the feeble invitation in Lennon's pop song: "You may say I'm a dreamer, but I'm not the only one; I hope some day you will join us, and the world will live as one." I don't know about you, but I would hate to stake the future of this country, and the well-being of my children and grandchildren and great-grandchildren, on a sentimental fancy worth about as much as the greeting card on which it belongs.

You, fellow believer, have the awesome opportunity to become a *real* change agent in your time. God has set before us an invitation, and it has nothing to do with the Pepsi generation who would like to teach the world to sing in perfect harmony. The *only* real thing is the gospel of Jesus Christ. The power for change in our time is nothing less than what Gideon received when the great "I AM" reduced his army to a paltry few before granting him victory over the vast hordes of his enemy.

In my previous book, *Real Homeland Security,* I have cited a "divine tipping point" as the threshold for the outpouring of God's blessings upon an America in which some divinely ordained number of Christians repent and seek healing for our country according to the conditions God set forth in 2 Chronicles 7:14. Malcolm Gladwell, the social scientist who coined this phrase to compare the dynamics of social change to the growth patterns of an infectious epidemic, describes this phenomenon in his book *The Tipping Point.*[10] "The law of the few" means that the epidemic begins with a very small group of exceptional people who are carriers of the infectious agent. The "stickiness factor" is the contagious nature of the virus itself. The rate of growth depends on whether the environment in which the virus spreads is either receptive or resistant to the infection.

Are you dismayed by the weight of the forces that are pulling this country down? I have good news for you: *the size of the problem does not govern the outcome.* God's divine tipping point does not depend on the masses of a godless culture—they are like the encampments of the Midianites. The "environment" in which the infectious agent of the gospel spreads starts with the church. Are God's people receptive or resistant to His call to repentance? Will they become agents of healing through humility and prayer? Will they seek God's face and turn from the wicked ways of the culture that has corrupted them? Will they become the exceptional few who spread an "epidemic" of revival?

We've all heard the phrase, "a journey of a thousand miles begins with a single step." That's what God is saying—it has to begin with *you.* If *you* will humble yourself and pray and seek His face and turn from your wicked ways, then God will forgive your sins and bring healing—and if *enough* individual Christians respond to God's call to repentance, then God will forgive their sins and bring healing to their land. We can't do this corporately: it has to be done one individual, one couple, one family at a time.

What does it truly mean to have a conversion experience with Christ—to be a believer? Christianity is not a religion. It is not an organization. It certainly has a world view, a philosophy, a set of core values—but it begins with a personal relationship.

World magazine publisher Joel Belz wrote a column a few months before the 2004 presidential election entitled "Downsizing—Maybe Christians haven't been thinking small enough." The builders of the Tower of Babel, he observed, were big dreamers who forgot about an even bigger God. Today, we have a government that pretends it can give us everything we need—so it is harder for Americans to sing "praise God, from whom all blessings flow."

Big government, big business, big entertainment organizations, big universities—even big churches—can divert our attention from an even bigger God, Belz cautions: "One definition of the secularizing of a culture is the extent to which that culture's people forget how big God is."[11] But "big" also distracts us from thinking small: It's easier to attend a protest march with thousands of other like-minded people than to sit down with a neighbor on the other side of the issue and have a conversation. It is more exciting to attend a mass evangelism event than to speak to a nonbelieving friend about Jesus. "Big" often means anonymous—and anonymity permits us to melt into the crowd instead of standing out to make a difference.

"A recurring theme in the Bible," writes Belz, "is that it is the task of God's servants to be faithful in small things—and then to trust a wise Father to assemble all those little matters into the accomplishment of His global purpose."[12]

No matter how hard you try to shelter yourself and your family, you can't hunker in the bunker and expect the world out there to go away.

Prepare to be impacted by your culture.

How many of us have had the experience of sending our children to Christian schools, where they meet other kids who come from supposedly Christian families, who are being negatively impacted by the culture? They end up taking drugs, engaging in premarital sex, getting married quickly and then getting divorced because they've been impacted by this culture. The only way to combat that influence is to be salt and light where you are. Withdrawal will never help.

If there are poisonous gases out there in the atmosphere of the culture, you can't help but breathe them. You can't wear a cultural gas mask all the time. You're going to breathe in that stage-three cultural smog, and it's going to make you more likely to succumb to lung cancer. But you have a choice whether you will be among the influencers or the influenced.

For authentic change to occur, it is not enough to have a change in behavior; there must be a change in nature. If we're going to have an America that is blessed by God, it will happen because some critical mass of Christians reaches some point of divine math in having this conversion experience—or those who have been converted get right with God. But it starts with individuals like you, accepting God's promise and believing God's promise that there *can* be a different future.

How will we know that we have reached a divine tipping point of God's blessing? We will know it when we look around and see an America that is espousing godly values—from within. Not from Washington; not from the state capitol; not from some restrictive social code; but because this is the consensus of the people.

Will you commit yourself to a vision of revival, awakening, and reformation for America? Will you accept the privilege of becoming one of the infectious few? Imagine a God-blessed America—it *can* happen here.

"HERE I AM; SEND ME"

Consider the example of William Carey, an outwardly ordinary Englishman whose zeal for the gospel spread to an impassioned concern that Christians take the good news of Christ to all people, all over the world.

Unlike Wilberforce, Carey had little formal training and no privileged upbringing. He came from a working-class family, leaving school at age twelve to become a cobbler's apprentice. Although he was brilliantly gifted in languages, when he was required to preach as a test of his candidacy for ordination, he initially flunked the exam. While pastoring a small Baptist congregation, he read *The Journals of Captain Cook,* which were thrilling the public with its tales of exotic adventures. Carey devoured these accounts as evidence of how desperately the peoples of the world needed Christ. While cobbling shoes as his day job, he kept books in front of him in order to master as many foreign languages as possible. In the quietness of his common labor, while reading his way around the world, his heart was pierced by the conviction that since all of humanity needed the gospel, those who were already entrusted with the gospel had the responsibility to make it known to all nations.

Carey's landmark book, *Enquiry Into the Obligations of the Christians to Use Means for the Conversion of the Heathen,* became a seminal work in the development of the modern missionary movement. He preached so powerfully on missions—with a clarion call to "expect great things of God; attempt great things for God"—that it led to the formation of the Particular Baptist Missionary Society. Shortly after that Carey departed for India, where he and his wife suffered severe tragedies (they lost three children; she lost her sanity) as they took the light of the gospel into the spiritual darkness of India. Despite overwhelming obstacles Carey persisted, and Christianity gained a foothold against the superstitious and cruel traditions of a Hindu culture. Carey's name is still revered today in India for the lasting impact of his social and educational reforms.

William Carey truly became God's torch to ignite the flame of the nineteenth-century churches' worldwide missionary expansion of the Christian faith.

I can't exaggerate how important *your* faith is to the future of this country. It doesn't matter where you come from, what your background is, or in what circumstances God has placed you. All that matters is the still small voice of your soul whispering to God, "Use me for Your purposes to bring healing to this land."

"It is not revolutions and upheavals that clear the road to new and better days," wrote poet Boris Pasternak, better known for authoring *Dr. Zhivago,* "but revelations, lavishness and torments of someone's soul, inspired and ablaze."[13]

In the quiet of your heart before God, ask him to bless America . . . through *you*. Perhaps you will help clear the road to new and better days as God inspires and inflames your soul with the desire to repent, and draw close to him, and seek healing for this land. Like Gideon, you may feel that you are the weakest and least likely member of God's family to accomplish great things for Him. But like William Carey, all you have to say is, "Here I am . . . send me." Expect great things from God. Attempt great things for God. God bless you . . . and in doing so, may God bless America.

· 3 ·

Imagine! A nation that affirms . . .

THE UNIQUE VALUE OF EVERY HUMAN LIFE

Imagine all the people . . . living life in peace . . . sharing all the world," wrote John Lennon. *Sounds pretty good,* people think. *Peace is a good thing. Sharing is a good thing. Let's make this our goal!*

In his book *Animal Liberation,*[14] which became the rallying flag for the animal rights movement, the controversial philosopher Peter Singer denounced the pain and suffering humans routinely cause to animals in the food industry and in scientific research. Indifference to such suffering is morally reprehensible, he contends. He calls such behavior "speciesism," a form of tyranny in which one species asserts its own self-interests at the expense of another. He likens it to racism and sexism on the grounds that it violates the principle that all living species have an equal right to be treated without cruelty and indifference.

Well, sure it's wrong for humans to treat animals as inanimate objects, some people reason. *Singer's right about that—let's join the cause!*

A highly influential public-interest organization promotes its cause with the statement, "If the rights of society's most vulnerable members are denied, everybody's rights are imperiled."[15] *Yes— a society's moral character can be judged by how well it looks out for the weak and neglected,* we might reason. Giving money to that organization would support important work!

Would it? Let's stop and take a closer look at these views. Yes, peace is a good thing. But how do we accomplish it? Will people stop fighting if we outlaw all weapons? Will nations quit waging war if they all agree to disarm? Yes, sharing is a good thing. But what does it look like? If the government declares that we no longer have a right to acquire personal property and make a profit, will that enforce sharing?

Peter Singer—a man whose moral compass has been completely demagnetized—wants us to care about the suffering we inflict on animals, because the interests of one species should not be elevated over the interests of another. When conflicts arise, he would resolve them by the criterion of the greater good. He believes that the interests of a few should not be given consideration over the interests of the many. As he explains:

> My broader credo can be found in *Practical Ethics,* 1st edn 1979, 2nd edn 1993. Here the treatment of animals receives its proper place, as one among several major ethical issues. I approach each

issue by seeking the solution that has the best consequences for all affected. By "best consequences,"
I understand that which satisfies the most *preferences*, weighted in accordance with the strength of
the preferences. Thus my ethical position is a form of
preference-utilitarianism.

In *Practical Ethics* I apply this ethic to such
issues as equality (both between humans, and
between humans and *non-human animals*), *abortion,
euthanasia and infanticide, the obligations of the
wealthy to those who are living in poverty,* the refugee
question, our interactions with non-human beings
and ecological systems, and obedience to the law.
A non-speciesist and *consequentialist* approach to
these issues leads to striking conclusions. It offers a
clear-cut account of why abortion is ethically justifi-
able, and an equally clear condemnation of our failure to share our wealth with people who are in
desperate need.

Some of my conclusions have been found shock-
ing, and not only in respect of animals. In Germany,
my advocacy of active euthanasia for severely
disabled newborn infants has generated heated
controversy. I first discussed this in *Practical Ethics;*
later, as co-author, with Helga Kuhse, in *Should the
Baby Live?*, 1985; and most recently in *Rethinking Life
and Death*, 1995. Perhaps it is only to be expected,
though, that there should be heated opposition to an

ethic that challenges the hitherto generally accepted ethical superiority of human beings, and the traditional view of the sanctity of human life.[16]

From animal rights to proactive euthanasia of human babies in just two paragraphs—how did he make *that* leap?

The same public-interest organization—the ACLU—dedicated to protecting the rights of the most vulnerable is also dedicated to protecting and advancing abortion rights. It is active in attempting to banish all traces of religion from the public arena. How did the ACLU arrive at *those* positions from its self-proclaimed concern for the vulnerable?

Let's go back to the word *imagine*—*imagine* what makes a person a person. *Imagine* the place of human beings in the universe. *Imagine* how we ought to live. Without a universal understanding of who we are and why we're here, all other issues might as well be left up to the imagination. A society without a clear definition of *life* cannot protect the sanctity of life. A culture without a true understanding of what it means to be human cannot value the worth of all human beings. A peace movement founded on an erroneous and poverty-stricken notion of human nature cannot induce human beings to make peace.

WHAT IS A HUMAN BEING?

The bottom-line reason why John Lennon and Peter Singer and the ACLU can start with goals that sound commendable yet ultimately lead to destructive and even heinous ends has everything to do with how they would answer the question, "What is a human being?" This is *the issue* at the root of the moral and ethical crisis in our country today.

John Lennon's view is based on a false premise that, first of all, there is no God: "Imagine there's no heaven, it's easy if you try, no hell below us, above us only sky." Therefore, there is no judgment. Second, human beings are basically good: "no need for greed or hunger, a brotherhood of man . . . sharing all the world." They are perfectible on their own. If they all work together, they can create a heaven on earth.

Sound familiar? The Bible records an event in early human history (Genesis 11:1–9) to which Lennon's lyrics bear an uncanny resemblance. The survivors of the great flood repopulated the earth and decided to make a name for themselves by building a city centered around a virtual staircase from earth to heaven, a great tower manifesting the unity and greatness of humankind. They would take history into their own hands, seize their own destiny, attain heavenly heights without God's help. This presumption has been humanity's downfall from the beginning of history.

The Devil incited human rebellion when he intruded on the Garden of Eden and said to our ancestors, "God doesn't want you to touch that forbidden fruit because He knows if you do this you'll be like God." Ever since, we've been swallowing the lie that human beings can become their own gods. We delude ourselves into thinking we can build a perfect society—and all of human history is heart-breaking testimony to the stark reality that we cannot.

The story of the Tower of Babel provides a picture of a society that believes there is neither heaven above it nor hell below it. We're born; we live; we die. No religion, no supernatural, no afterlife. No accountability. Lennon's view is simply another variation on the attempt to construct a Tower of Babel.

Peter Singer takes this view of life on earth a step further. If there is nothing sacred about the human race, then neither is there anything sacred about individual human lives. If the common good means that a few must be sacrificed for the many, then sacrificing a few can be a good thing. We can even choose to decide who is a person and who isn't. Then we can justify the elimination of the few by declaring that they aren't *really* people, anyway:

> Only a person can want to go on living, or have plans for the future, because only a person can even understand the possibility of a future existence for herself or himself. This means that to end the lives of people, against their will, is different from ending the lives of beings who are not people. Indeed, strictly speaking, in the case of those who are not people, we cannot talk of ending their lives against or in accordance with their will, because they are not capable of having a will on such a matter. . . . [Killing] a person against her or his will is a much more serious wrong than killing a being that is not a person. If we want to put this in the language of rights, then it is reasonable to say that only a person has a right to life.[17]

Singer's view does not distinguish between humans and animals on a moral plane, because humans are simply one of many species. To elevate the interests of the human species over the interests of animal species is immoral, therefore. Singer's view is one logical extension of the belief that life happened by accident and human beings have no special place or purpose in the universe.

The ACLU defines the "vulnerable" by a politically driven agenda based on a pick-and-choose menu of needs. Underlying their activities is virtually the same view of human beings that drove construction of the Tower of Babel: humans are the center of the universe, without accountability to any transcendent authority. Therefore the ACLU focuses its attention on protection *from* religion, not *for* religion. It insists that an unborn child is not a human being but the material property of the woman carrying it. Because we are free of accountability to anyone or anything beyond ourselves, we can dismiss the life growing within her as a material burden to be eliminated instead of recognizing it as an unborn, and therefore vulnerable, person in need of protection.

Our country was founded on the belief that life is sacred. The Declaration of Independence is based upon this "self-evident" truth: " . . . that all men are created equal, that they are endowed by their Creator with certain unalienable rights. . . . " As President George W. Bush remarked, "The right to life does not come from government; it comes from the Creator of life."[18] American culture has increasingly abandoned this belief, losing its moral compass. We have become like the Israelites during the time of the judges: "In those days there was no king in Israel; every man did what was right in his own eyes" (Judges 17:6 NASB).

THE MEANING OF BEING HUMAN

Are human beings simply specks of cosmic dust blown on the winds of fate? Is there no meaning or purpose to existence? Or have we been created with a plan for our lives? Are we just another species alongside the animal kingdom, or are we made in the image of God?

David, the shepherd-king of Israel, gives us the answer in a lyrical and beautiful description of our place in the universe: "O LORD, our Lord, how majestic is your name in all the earth! You have set your glory above the heavens," he marvels. "When I consider your heavens, the work of your fingers, the moon and the stars, which you have set in place, what is man that you are mindful of him, the son of man that you care for him?" he asks, marveling that the Creator of such a vast universe would stoop to lavish His attention on frail human beings. "You made him a little lower than the heavenly beings and crowned him with glory and honor. You made him ruler over the works of your hands; you put everything under his feet: all flocks and herds, and the beasts of the field, the birds of the air, and the fish of the sea, all that swim the paths of the seas" (Psalm 8:1, 3–8).

"Man is the special creation of God, made in His own image," Christians affirm.[19] God never created a nobody—everybody is a somebody. We have a destiny to fulfill, not only for today but also for all eternity. God created us for a reason, and it makes a dramatic difference here on earth whether we pay attention to that reason or ignore it. It will make an even more dramatic difference in eternity.

What difference does it make when a society believes that everybody is a somebody? We know all too well what a society looks like when its values are shaped by the belief that not everybody is a somebody, and a somebody who gets in the way becomes a nobody. *Time* columnist Charles Krauthammer described this picture when he scolded the Democrats for exploiting the issue of

stem-cell research during the 2004 presidential campaign, cyni-
cally suggesting that we were on the cusp of miraculous cures if
only President George W. Bush would stop playing politics with it.

During the Democratic convention in August, Ron Reagan, son
of the late president Ronald Reagan, gave a speech from the plat-
form in support of stem-cell research. Rather than acknowledging
that the issue presents a complex moral challenge, Reagan demo-
nized those opposed to it. As Krauthammer wrote:

> In an election year, it is too much to expect
> serious and complicated moral issues to be treated
> with seriousness and complexity. Nonetheless, the
> Democrats have managed to caricature and debase
> the debate over embryonic stem-cell research . . . .
> Having no doubt discovered through focus groups
> and polling that stem-cell research might be a useful
> reverse-wedge issue against Republicans, who have
> traditionally enjoyed an electoral advantage on "val-
> ues," the Democrats showcased it with a prime-time
> convention speech by the well-known medical
> expert Ron Reagan. Message? On the one side are the
> forces of good, on the verge of curing such terrible
> afflictions as Parkinson's, diabetes and spinal-cord
> injury. On the other are the forces of reaction and
> superstition who, slaves to a primitive religiosity,
> would condemn millions to suffer and die. Or as
> Reagan subtly put it, the choice is "between reason
> and ignorance, between true compassion and mere
> ideology." . . . When I was 22 and a first-year

medical student, I suffered a spinal-cord injury. I have not walked in 32 years. I would be delighted to do so again. But not at any price. I think it is more important to bequeath to my son a world that retains a moral compass, a world that when unleashing the most powerful human discovery since Alamogordo—something as protean, elemental, powerful and potentially dangerous as the manipulation and re-formation of the human embryo—recognizes that lines must be drawn and fences erected.[20]

This is a clear example of pick-and-choose morality when the littlest somebodies in the world are dismissed as nobodies, standing in the way of progress.

Imagine a society in which most people really believe that human beings are intended for eternity, and this life is not all there is. That's a society that will welcome every human being into life, regardless of physical or mental abnormality or ethnicity or the circumstances of conception. It is a society that will value each human being simply for being human, honoring the truth that we are made in God's image.

Let's turn the tide. God has already given us the guidelines for what to believe and how to live: "I will instruct you and teach you in the way you should go; I will counsel you and watch over you. Do not be like the horse or the mule, which have no understanding but must be controlled by bit and bridle or they will not come to you" (Psalm 32:8–9). God speaks to us so we can hear Him, so we can understand and obey. Imagine a society that values the sanctity of every human life—starting with you.

Good News, Bad News

Here's the good news and the bad news for our culture. The good news is that because we are the special creation of God, we are not the prisoners of our environment. We are free to make choices. We can experience meaning and purpose in life.

The bad news is that for every choice we make, there is a consequence—now and in eternity. We can't blame our genetics or our upbringing for our behavior because in Christ we can overcome them. And we can't escape our accountability for our choices, because the soul is immortal and after death we're going to continue living, in one place or the other.

In a world that is bounded by heaven above and hell below, each person is a special creation of God, responsible before Him and of enormous value to Him. But as Rick Warren says in his phenomenally successful book *The Purpose-Driven Life*,[21] it's not about you. It's about God. It's about serving a purpose greater than yourself. The good news is that there is no purposeless or meaningless life. The bad news for those who want to believe in human autonomy is that we don't get to choose the purpose or the meaning. We just get to discover it. God is the one who gives our lives purpose. God is the one who endows our lives with meaning.

One of the biggest areas of confusion over meaning and purpose in our culture today is gender. Consider the following philosophy:

> Though our culture tends to group characteris-
> tics into "masculine" and "feminine," many people
> find some amount of gender transgression exciting,
> so there is some crossover between the two cate-
> gories. Ultimately, gender is a "mix and match" mode

of self-expression, and people within our culture are ever finding new ways to express their gender, with exciting subtleties and intriguing implications. In general, it works best to think of all effects—sexual orientation, gender identity, sexual identity, and any others—as varying along a continuous spectrum of self-expression, rather than in just one of two or three ways. Sexual orientation, gender identity, and sexual identity are independent of each other. A person may express any variation of each of these in any combination. To discourage the free expression of identity and orientation by an individual is to impose a damaging burden of conformity.

Sexual Orientation is which sex you find erotically attractive: opposite (hetero), same (homo), or both (bi). *Sexual Identity* is how you see yourself physically: male, female, or in between. If someone is born female, but wishes to see their body as male in all respects, their sexual identity is male. It is generally rude to speak of such a person as female, since it denies their right to inhabit the social and physical role of their choosing. . . . *Gender Identity* is how you see yourself socially: man, woman, or a combination of both. One may have [male anatomy] but prefer to relate socially as a woman, or one may have [female anatomy] but prefer to relate as a man. One might prefer to be fluid, relating sometimes as a man and sometimes as a woman. Or one might not identify as either one, relating androgynously.[22]

Contrary to such popular thinking, gender is not a by-product of the reproduction of species. It is a divine creation with powerful meaning and purpose: "Man is the special creation of God, made in His own image. *He created them male and female* as the crowning work of His creation. *The gift of gender* is thus part of the goodness of God's creation."[23]

When we deny the sanctity of all life, we rob gender of its intended purpose and meaning. When we distort gender, it leads to distorted thinking and practice regarding our sexuality. And without a healthy understanding and practice of sexuality, we distort what it means to be human—perhaps the gravest moral issue facing our country today.

· 4 ·

Imagine! An American culture in which . . .

SEXUALITY IS HONORED, NOT DEGRADED

Who would ever dream of featuring in a championship foot-ball game halftime show watched by an estimated 140 million people, many of them in family settings, two pop stars known for their sexually explicit lyrics and suggestive performances? In February 2004, executives at CBS and MTV did just that. The performance took a decidedly pornographic turn when the male star ripped off a strategically placed section of his female partner's bodice. The incident provoked public outcry and a hefty FCC fine. Perhaps it should not have been such a surprise—after all, the singer was simply acting out the lyrics of a song already on the music best-seller charts. This incident was just one more descending step in the downward spiral of popular entertainment.

What if we lived in a culture in which this kind of scenario would never have arisen at all? Imagine if our culture's idea of a championship halftime show included an attractively but modestly dressed female musician who performed without salacious dance moves, and a male singer who crooned songs absent of lyrics about preying on women for cheap thrills, who had not earned his fifteen seconds of fame through highly publicized conquests of female entertainment stars.

Imagine a generation of young girls growing up without constant exposure to the debauchery (and publicly announced deflowering) of female pop singers as models of womanhood. Imagine a generation of young men reaching the age of sexual maturity without the widespread cultural influence of porn purveyors such as Hugh Hefner and Larry Flynt, without endless product commercials selling sex to define their brands . . . young men who had learned self-control and self-respect through encouragement to live up to their best rather than instant gratification through license to live down to their worst impulses.

Imagine a culture that had so marginalized depravity to the utter fringes of society that any individual choosing to indulge in it had to exert great effort, and risk social censure, just to obtain access to it.

Several years ago, with funding assistance from the Disney Corporation, New York City (under then-mayor Rudolf Giuliani) conducted a clean-up campaign of Times Square to eliminate its sleaze shows and refashion the area as a family-friendly tourist mecca and revitalized theater district. Many of the sex shops were closed down or moved out to Brooklyn and Queens, but some of them were simply shifted a few blocks west, remaining within easy reach of the tourist trade.

Although the effort was widely applauded, it sparked protest among some who lamented the loss of the historic "character" of Times Square. New York University Press published a book on this development by celebrated essayist, award-winning science fiction writer, and distinguished professor of comparative literature at U Mass.-Amherst—Samuel Delaney. Delaney's work, *Times Square Red, Times Square Blue,* was praised by critics for its thesis that corporate greed, not community concern, had largely driven the urban make-over, destroying the area's vitality and diversity. But in making this case, Delaney chose to chronicle his intimate personal history of frequenting porn shows and sleaze shops. He described his homosexual experiences with working-class and homeless men to lament the loss of urban areas promoting social interaction across lines of class, race, and sexual orientation. Red-light districts can be beneficial, Delaney maintained, because they foster social coherence and empathy.

Realize that this paean to pornography was not a magazine article by a hack journalist writing for some independent rag. It was presented as a serious and substantive work of anthropological insight, social commentary, and memoir. Yet it contained revelations that decades earlier would have resulted in the loss of the author's prestigious position and reputation. In many social circles, it served to legitimize, even praise, the sex industry.

Have we fallen so far that our models of community life have been reduced to the breeding-pens of furtive and exploitative acts that human beings inflict on one another to their mutual destruction? Sadly enough, apparently so.

Let us imagine an America that would never think of extolling pornography at *any* level of society or form of expression . . . a world in which you would not have to monitor what your children watched on television, listened to on the radio, saw on videos at their friends' houses, viewed on movie screens, and downloaded on computer screens . . . a world in which multiple channels of entertainment and recreation streamed clean content into our homes and work venues and places of leisure.

Let us imagine living in this culture and ask, "Why *not* an America like this?"

Does this proposal sound to you like so much pie in the sky? Are you thinking that one person, or a handful of people, cannot turn the tide of an entire culture?

To understand how the power of one person helped drag our country down to its current state within a few short decades, consider a sobering history lesson from earlier in the twentieth century, which is coming round again in these early years of the twenty-first century.

MEET "DR. SEX"

If you were under forty entering the twenty-first century you probably didn't know much about the name Kinsey, if you had even heard it at all—although as of November 2004 that is likely to have changed with the release of the major motion picture *Kinsey,* featuring international film star Liam Neeson as sex researcher Dr. Alfred C. Kinsey.

Those of us who came of age in the 1950s, 1960s, and early 1970s were heirs to the social legacy of the *Kinsey Reports*, purportedly scientific studies of sexuality published in two books, *Sexual Behavior in the Human Male* (1948) and *Sexual Behavior in the Human Female* (1953). With initial funding from the Rockefeller Foundation, the studies were conducted by Dr. Alfred C. Kinsey, a zoologist (watch for the connections) at Indiana University, originally in preparation for a course designed for married or engaged students. Dr. Kinsey had previously specialized in research of the gall wasp, and when he turned to "the human animal" he began with the presupposition that sex is a purely physiological response. The only difference in sexual behavior between the animal kingdom and the human animal, he contended, was that animals had sex only to procreate.

Kinsey conducted his research with the driving belief that sexual acts were inherently morally neutral. He contended that much of what was considered sexual deviancy was actually widespread practice, which should be accepted as normative behavior. Kinsey showed himself an heir of Sigmund Freud in his belief that social repression of sexuality is a damaging constraint on a fundamental human drive. In other words, sexual impulses need to be indulged, not censored or controlled. To defend this thesis Kinsey announced findings such as these:

- Sexual activity among American males was so widespread and diverse that 95 percent of them qualified as sex offenders under prevailing laws.
- Male homosexuality in the 16–55 age group constituted 10 percent of the population.

- Premarital sex was found to be helpful preparation for many women entering marriage.
- Most men and nearly half of all women had been sexually active before marriage.
- Half of all men and nearly half of all women had committed adultery.
- Of women who had committed adultery, nearly three-quarters of them felt it had not hurt their marriage, and a small percentage even felt that it had helped.
- Nearly three-quarters of all men had experience with prostitutes.
- Nearly all single women, and a quarter of married women, reported having had abortions, and most of those abortions were performed by professional physicians.
- Children and even infants are capable of having sexual experiences and would be sexually active if it weren't for societal inhibitions and cultural censure, and sexual encounters between adults and children are not by definition harmful.
- Nearly one-fifth of all males growing up on farms had experienced sex with animals, and bestiality was simply another garden variety of human sexuality.
- Sexuality itself is a spectrum of human behavior with bisexuality as the most balanced state and at either end, heterosexuality and homosexuality.

Kinsey presented "evidence" of these findings as scientific information, intended to provide needed correctives to what he considered the irrational and damaging moralism of his day. Kinsey's opinions became so influential that they triggered widespread and lasting changes in law, education, and popular beliefs based on the supposed "science" of human sexuality.

When Kinsey's first report was published to widespread acclaim, it sold two hundred thousand copies in the first two months. Kinsey was dubbed "Dr. Sex" in the popular media, who praised him for his courage in taking on the moral establishment and compared him to researchers such as Galileo, Darwin, and Freud. *Playboy* founder Hugh Hefner and sex therapist "Dr. Ruth" Westheimer trace their roots to the ground Kinsey plowed. Kinsey's conclusions became so mainstreamed in American culture and higher education that Indiana University continues to carry forward the work through the Kinsey Institute for Research in Sex, Gender, and Reproduction.

However, Kinsey's work was—and has remained—controversial not only because his findings departed so radically from prevailing social mores, but also because his methodology fell so far short of generally accepted criteria for sound scientific research. Conspicuous dissenters from the fawning crowds included such notables as Margaret Mead, Abraham Maslow, Dr. Karl Menninger, and Lionel Trilling, all of whom had grave concerns about flaws in Kinsey's methodology.

For example, Kinsey was criticized for interviewing prisoners, pedophiles, prostitutes, and sexually abused children among his research subjects and then extrapolating those findings to the general population. His research into male sexuality was based largely on subjects who had volunteered for the study instead of being selected at random from the population at large. Outraged critics demanded to know how he had gathered research on children and infants—such as what triggered their sexual orgasms and how long they lasted—without committing sexual assault upon them. As the forthcoming *Kinsey* movie will explore, the image of dispassionate scientist and stable, married man was belied by revelations that Kinsey's research involved multiple sexual encounters—bisexual, voyeuristic, and sadomasochistic—involving himself, his wife, and his own staff. As the volume of criticism grew louder, the Rockefeller Foundation withdrew its grant of $100,000 per year.

Early responses to the movie indicate another social showdown between Kinsey critics and supporters. Longtime critic and pornography researcher Judith Reisman, Ph.D., wrote a public letter to Liam Neeson protesting his decision to portray Kinsey and citing documentation to support her contention that Kinsey inflicted horrific sexual abuse upon children in the course of conducting his "junk science." Multiple nonprofit organizations advocating sexual abstinence and family values are protesting the movie because they believe it glamorizes Kinsey as a hero and perpetuates myths about his research.

On the other side of the showdown is this observation from *Kinsey* writer-director Bill Condon, who won an Oscar for his movie *Gods and Monsters* (about gay Hollywood film director James "Frankenstein" Whale): "We all owe a tremendous debt to him. There's a really direct line from the books that he published, to the sexual revolution of the 1960s, to a lot of the freedoms that we enjoy today." Commenting to journalists at the film's debut in the September 2004 Toronto Film Festival, he went on to say, "Kinsey is a forgotten figure, so I'm hoping that this movie can sort of shed new light on him." When asked about protests of the movie, Liam Neeson waved off the issue by commenting, "Sex is controversial. It always has been; it always will be."[24]

In his coverage of the Toronto Film Festival, *Variety* reporter Jeffrey Hodgson revealed his own bias in favor of Kinsey by tossing a nod to the controversy while failing to disclose the critical flaws in Kinsey's scientific methodology:

> Kinsey burst onto the public scene in the late 1940s with release of "Sexual Behavior in the Human Male," one of the first major scientific studies of human sexuality. The work shattered many misconceptions and got the public talking about the taboo subject. But the scientist also drew fire from many religious and traditional-values groups who thought his work was immoral and dangerous.[25]

You would never know from this bit of journalism that Kinsey's "scientific studies" drew fire from respected authorities well outside the "traditional values" camp. Nor would you know that the movie itself reveals that Kinsey involved his own family and staff in sexual experiments that even by today's permissive standards would likely get him fired, discredited, and criminally charged.

A TRAGIC LEGACY

Kinsey admirers are loath to acknowledge the critics because they want to champion, rather than call into question the Kinsey-inspired sexual revolution of the 1960s and its aftermath. I am not claiming a direct line of cause-and-effect from Kinsey's research to the immorality plaguing our society. But multiple connections can be traced in an unbroken chain from the Kinsey reports to major influences driving the sexual confusion and degradation of our day.

Here is an example of the kind of sexual education thousands of young women today are receiving on a daily basis. It is loudly applauded as healthy teaching about sexuality, and it is considered normative by many people in our courts and public school system:

> Our society does not help a woman understand
> her real feelings about sex. Thinking about your
> answers to each of these questions may help you
> understand some of yours:
> What are my sexual desires?
> What are my sexual limits—am I clear with
> myself about what I will do and won't do?
> Do I want to have sex?
> What do I want to get out of it?
> Will I get what I want?
> What does my partner want? Why?
> Could I get hurt?
> Will this relationship be honest, equal, respectful,
> and responsible?
> Am I prepared for any physical or emotional
> outcome? [26]
> *Not all women are interested in sexual relationships*
> *with men.* They may be interested in relationships
> with other women. No one knows for sure what
> makes women lesbian, bisexual, or heterosexual.
> We do know that people don't decide their sexual

orientations. Our sexual identities develop as natu-
rally as the rest of what makes us who we are.[27]

Consider a few statistics on sexually active teenagers from The
Alan Guttmacher Institute—a nonprofit research firm with histor-
ical roots in Planned Parenthood and a mission that reflects the
Planned Parenthood agenda:

- By their 18th birthday, 6 in 10 teenage women and nearly
  7 in 10 teenage men have had sexual intercourse.[28]
- A sexually active teenager who does not use contraception
  has a 90 % chance of becoming pregnant within a year.[29]
- Although the pregnancy rate among U. S. women aged
  15–19 declined steadily in the 1990s, analysis of the
  teenage pregnancy rate decline between 1988 and 1995
  found that approximately one-quarter of the decline was
  due to delayed onset of sexual intercourse among
  teenagers, while 75 percent was due to the increased use of
  highly effective and long-acting contraceptive methods
  among sexually experienced teenagers.[30]
- Despite the decline, the United States continues to have
  one of the highest teenage pregnancy rates in the developed world—twice as high as those in England, Wales, or
  Canada and nine times as high as rates in the Netherlands
  and Japan.[31]
- Every year, roughly 4 million new sexually transmitted dis-
  ease (STD) infections occur among teenagers in the United
  States. Compared with rates among teens in other developed countries, rates of gonorrhea and chlamydia among
  U. S. teenagers are extremely high.[32]

Another indicator of the Kinsey legacy in our culture is Cornell University Library's Human Sexuality Collection (HSC), a gathering of materials on sexuality, popular science, and culture with a stated primary focus on homosexuality and the politics of pornography. The HSC charts an explosion of popular books on sexuality in the 1960s consisting primarily of "case histories, studies in sexual perversion, stated 'exposés' of 'the homosexual underground,' and explicit how-to books. Many feature sexually explicit photographs and illustrations. Common topics include lesbianism, male homosexuality, transsexuality, sex offenders, 'sexual perversion' (anal and oral sex, fetishes, masturbation, sadomasochism, bestiality, etc.), and sex in marriage."[33]

One of the most disturbing indicators of our culture's rush to moral ruin is the landmark study on pornography undertaken by the Attorney General's Commission on Pornography in the mid-1980s. Under President Ronald Reagan's directive, then-Attorney General Edwin Meese III convened the commission in order to "determine the nature, extent, and impact on society of pornography in the United States" and make recommendations for containing the spread of pornography.[34]

We will take a look at this report in greater depth in the next two chapters, but for our purposes here one particular passage from the report sufficiently illuminates its grim content. When the final report was released, each of the commission members contributed a personal statement summarizing his or her response to the study process and results. Commissioner Diane D. Cusack, a graduate of the Harvard Business School experienced in market research analysis and a leader in community affairs and public health issues, sounded a warning about "stemming the tide of obscenity which is flooding our environment":

> There is no doubt among us that the quantity of pornography available today in America is almost overwhelming. In addition, that large portion of it which would be obscene under the Miller test [the Supreme Court's 1973 ruling in *Miller v. California* setting standards for defining obscene materials unprotected by the First Amendment] is shockingly violent, degrading and perverted. It is my personal opinion that there is no one who is a consistent user of this material who is not harmed by it. And who, in turn, may harm others because of it. This obscene material should be prosecuted vigorously.[35]

WHO WILL CREATE A NEW LEGACY?

Can it be any clearer that the most critical battle lines we face today are over sexuality? The crisis boils down to one essential foundation: If there is a God and we are His creation, then God is the one who lays down the rules for who we are as sexual beings and how we are to receive the gift of our sexuality. If there is not a God who made us in His image, if there is no eternal destiny for our souls, then we're free to define ourselves sexually. That leads to the tragic cultural value dominating our view of life: *if it feels good, do it.*

So then, why not homosexuality? Why not polygamy? Why not bestiality? We have people arguing for every possible perversion of God's design for sex. And even though the church is outwardly drawing the battle lines in the sand, inwardly the reality is that sexuality is a far bigger and more troubling issue in the church than abortion. There are a lot of believers who would never have an abortion, but they have affairs. There are even more Christian young people who would never have an affair, but they will sleep together before they get married. And tragically, many Christians have become involved in, or addicted to, pornography—the deadly cancer that has wrapped itself around the vital organs of our national life.

Paul described what happens in a culture when it throws off sexual restraint, drowning out the voice of conscience in full-blown sexual rebellion:

> Therefore God gave them over in the sinful
> desires of their hearts to sexual impurity for the
> degrading of their bodies with one another. They
> exchanged the truth of God for a lie, and worshiped
> and served created things rather than the Creator—
> who is forever praised. Amen.
>
> Because of this, God gave them over to shameful
> lusts. Even their women exchanged natural relations
> for unnatural ones. In the same way the men also
> abandoned natural relations with women and were
> inflamed with lust for one another. Men committed
> indecent acts with other men, and received in them-
> selves the due penalty for their perversion.

Furthermore, since they did not think it worthwhile to retain the knowledge of God, he gave them over to a depraved mind, to do what ought not to be done. They have become filled with every kind of wickedness, evil, greed and depravity. They are full of envy, murder, strife, deceit and malice. They are gossips, slanderers, God-haters, insolent, arrogant and boastful; they invent ways of doing evil; they disobey their parents; they are senseless, faithless, heartless, ruthless. Although they know God's righteous decree that those who do such things deserve death, they not only continue to do these very things but also approve of those who practice them. (Romans 1:24–32)

If Alfred Kinsey, a psychologically confused and morally compromised man who died prematurely at age sixty-two—a result, many have theorized, of the consequences brought on by his increasingly bizarre personal behavior—could wield such influence in our country, what could be done by individual Christians who committed themselves to repentance and renewal, personally and corporately?

Think of it: the America God would bless would be a society in which crimes of sexual violence would be rare. Women could walk the streets without fear. Young women could pursue their studies and enjoy social activities on college campuses without undue risk because crimes of sexual violence against women and crimes of sexual violence against boys and girls would be very rare. We know from established research that hard-core pornography is the engine that drives the increase in crimes of sexual violence against women and children. Of sexual perpetrators in prison, 75 to 78 percent viewed pornography within twenty-four hours of committing their crimes. Nearly half of them had pornography on their person or in their car at the time they perpetrated the crimes.

An America that has been blessed by God would reflect a biblical understanding of sexuality suffusing the society like salt and light. God would be pouring out His blessing upon just and unjust alike, so there would be laws to eradicate pornography as well as laws that severely punish sexual criminals.

Half of all rapes are committed by repeat offenders. If we didn't let rapists out of prison, or if we forced them to be physically or chemically castrated, we would cut the rape rate in half, right then and there. The America blessed by God would no longer be plagued by pornography, so crimes of sexual violence against women and children would be driven down to an infinitesimally small number.

I can't entirely grasp the difference this would make because I'm a man. But I have a wife and two adult daughters, so I am sensitized to the fact that a woman's lack of feeling safe impacts what she does, where she goes, when she goes, and how she feels about going there in a way that I do not experience. My wife and daughters don't go to the shopping mall late in the evening unless I can go with them because they don't want to go in and out of the parking lot by themselves.

A fear of violent attack is always a calculating factor for how women live their lives, twenty-four hours a day. Imagine what it would be like if that were not the case. How many opportunities could it open up for women? How would they feel about their lives if they no longer suffered from being dehumanized as sexual appliances, because society had virtually eliminated the predatory, self-gratifying sexuality that is created and fed by the Internet's endless supply of hard-core pornography?

It takes a while to get your mind around the difference that would make in our society. I think that's a difference worth pursuing.

We are suffering the devastating consequences of a sorry chapter in American history. Who will write the next one? Where is the next leading sexologist who can redress the harm we have inherited from Alfred Kinsey? Where will the next Dr. Ruth come from, and who will have mentored her—another Kinsey heir, or a Christian with the highest standards of scientific research and personal conduct both publicly and privately? Who is taking a stand against pornography . . . in our homes, in the company our children keep, in defense of the victims not just who view it, but who are forced to make it?

Why *not* an America in which Dr. Kinsey is discredited and Indiana University is compelled to dismantle the Kinsey Institute?

Let us visualize what might be: specifically, a culture that nurtures marriage instead of undermining it. Why *not* an America in which one of the greatest causes of marital strife and brokenness has been largely eliminated?

· 5 ·

Imagine! An America in which . . .

STABLE AND HAPPY MARRIAGES ARE THE NORM

During President George W. Bush's first term, I was privileged to be part of a luncheon on November 12, 2002, at the Justice Department. Those attending included Dr. James Dobson of Focus on the Family and Charles Colson of Prison Fellowship. When Attorney General Ashcroft asked each of us to name what we felt was the single greatest threat facing America, I think we were all a little surprised that each of us had a different answer.

"Until a few years ago, I would have said without hesitation that the greatest single threat facing America is the sanctity of human life," I offered, "starting with abortion and moving out to the culture of death that it has engendered, the killing of already-born babies, the killing of partially born babies, the push for physician-assisted suicide, for allowing others the right to withhold feeding from coma patients, even the right to withhold sustenance from prematurely born babies. This whole 'culture of death,' as Pope John Paul II has called it, has devalued life and set minimum standards people have to meet in order to earn what is naturallly a God-given right to life—a right upon which our nation was founded.

"I recently changed my mind, not because the sanctity of human life issues has gotten any better, but it has been overtaken by hard-core pornography and its full-blown offensive for a fully pagan sexuality in which anything goes. I believe hard-core Internet pornography is destroying more lives every day than the four-thousand killed each day through abortion."

Chuck Colson said he hated to disagree but that he believed the greatest problem facing America today is still the denial of the sanctity of life. He offered a strong rendition of the horrors of how human life is being cheapened through developments such as abortion, assisted suicide, cloning, stem-cell research, and a whole complex of issues radiating from this key battleground.

Jim Dobson then declared he felt Chuck and I were both mistaken and that the single greatest threat to America is the whole assault on marriage, led by the radical homosexual movement. He argued that it is attempting to redefine out of existence the basic building block of society from the beginning of human history. If that goes, all is lost, he maintained, and went into an eloquent defense of the family.[36]

Actually, from the perspective of 2005, it would seem all three of us were right. Pornography, the culture of death, and a radical homosexual assault on marriage are the three modern Horsemen of the Apocalypse, wreaking havoc and destruction across the landscape of twenty-first-century America.

We live in a society that has reduced sexuality to one more self-gratifying right of individual choice—if you want it, you should be able to have it, and nobody should stand in your way of getting it. The gay marriage agenda is attempting to redefine our core institution of family and community by dismantling the moral foundation that has given our nation stability and strength. The pornography industry is capitalizing on unprecedented access to drag as many people as possible down into its addictive black hole.

Imagine a society in which human beings accepted their masculinity and femininity and understood that those are equal but not the same, that they were created to complement one another, not to compete with one another—and not to be obliterated or neglected as if they didn't exist. Here is the supreme area of conflict in our culture: how the purpose and meaning of human life is expressed in our sexuality. It is certainly the supreme area of conflict in the Christian church. Fighting that conflict is an inside-out effort. It starts with the individual, then the family, and then the community.

One of the most visible effects of the damage done by this sexual rebellion is the debilitated state of marriage in our culture. Marriage is under attack as never before. The divorce rate is the same outside the church as it is inside the church. The rate of cohabitation prior to marriage, or as an alternative to marriage, continues to rise.

What can we do to reverse these trends? Better still, what we can do—not to return to the way it used to be, but to move forward into a future we have never seen? Let us start with some eye-opening studies about marriage and divorce.

IS DIVORCE EVER AN ALTERNATIVE TO MARRIAGE?

If you were to take an informal survey of couples who have been married for at least twenty years or more, I am sure that most of them would agree that it is more difficult to maintain a healthy marriage today than it was two decades ago. The cultural environment exerts tremendous pressures on husbands and wives. And it doesn't help that our society bombards us with the message to take the easy way out: divorce.

One of the biggest lies propagated by our culture is that divorce is an acceptable option if your marriage doesn't turn out the way you hoped. In fact, if you feel unhappy, the lie goes, you are better off getting divorced than staying in an unhappy marriage. (In this context, I use the phrase "unhappy marriage" to refer to a marriage with conflict for reasons other than violent abuse, which is an entirely different category and needs to be treated as such.)

A landmark study published in July 2002 from the Institute for American Values looked at spouses who rated their marriages as unhappy and then were interviewed again five years later to find out what had happened. Some had divorced or separated, and some had stayed married. Six nationally known family scholars from major universities, appointed by the institute, combined their findings in a report entitled "Does Divorce Make People

Happy? Findings from a Study of Unhappy Marriages."[37] These are not theologians or preachers; these are social and hard scientists. They wanted to compare the findings with the conventional wisdom that if you are in an unhappy marriage you have two choices: stay married and be miserable, or get divorced and find relief—or even future happiness.

The report contrasted unhappy spouses who had divorced or separated with unhappy spouses who had remained married. Those who had divorced or separated were no happier than those who had remained married. Divorced spouses who had remarried did not generally improve their happiness; only one out of five who had remarried felt happy in the new marriage. This is not difficult math here. If you're unhappy in your marriage and you divorce and remarry, you have only a one in five chance of being happily remarried five years later. Divorce does not reduce symptoms of depression; it does not raise self-esteem; it does not provide a greater sense of personal mastery over one's life.

One surprising finding was that among those who were unhappily married but stayed married anyway, two out of three ended up feeling happily married five years later. So if you are unhappy now in your marriage, your chances of being happy five years from now are *much greater* simply if you *stay married*—and that's not even factoring in how much brighter the outlook would be if you and your spouse were Christians!

Are you thinking that I don't realize *how* unhappy a marriage you may be in right now? Here is encouraging news for you: the worst marriages in this study usually had the most dramatic turnarounds, overcoming extended periods of marital conflict for serious reasons such as alcoholism, infidelity, verbal abuse, emotional neglect, depression, illness, and work reversals. Counseling was seldom cited as a major factor in the turnaround. (If the conflict featured damaging behavior by the husband, the marriage tended to improve not through counseling, but by the wife's tendency to seek help from others in pressuring the husband to change his behavior.)

Perhaps most surprising was that marriages with such serious difficulties improved not because the two spouses resolved the problems, but because they outlasted them. The passage of time had eased the sources of conflict and distress, and playing a major role was their belief in the importance of staying married—and their support from friends and family who also placed high value on marriages that endure.

Reasons why these spouses chose *not* to divorce include children's need for fathers, the financial strain of divorce, marriage vows, religious convictions, family values, friendships, and the personal love story underlying the marriage. Outweighing the stresses were benefits such as companionship through good times and bad, partnership in raising kids, personal support, family togetherness, and a sense of personal stability.

WOMEN, YOU HAVE MORE POWER THAN YOU MAY REALIZE

The strength of marriage in our country has been eroded as those benefits appear to fade in light of fleeting enticements such as cohabitation, one of the single greatest sabotages of marriage in our day. The National Marriage Project (NMP) studied mating and marrying behavior over the final four decades of the twentieth century and issued its findings in 2002 in the "State of Our Unions" Report.[38] Over this period, marriage declined dramatically as a status of parenthood and as an experience for couples living together for the first time.

The popular gender stereotype about marriage is that women want it but men don't. The NMP found evidence that this is, in fact, reality. Here are the top ten reasons why men are more reluctant than women to commit to marriage:

10. They want to enjoy single life as long as they can.

9. They want to have a house before they have a wife.

8. They are reluctant to marry a woman who already has children.

7. They are relatively free of social pressures to marry.

6. Their perfect soul mate has not yet appeared.

5. They don't want to deal with the changes and compromises they think marriage will require.

4. They want to wait until they are older to have children.

3. They want to avoid the costs and complications of divorce.

2. They can live with a woman and enjoy the benefits of a wife without having to marry her.

And the number one reason why men are reluctant to commit to marriage is . . .

1. They can get sex outside of marriage far more easily than ever.

As Charles Colson put it, "Grandma was right: Men won't buy the cow if they can get the milk free."[39] It sounds crude, but then the reality is even cruder. Many disillusioned girls and women have suffered the consequences of the generalization that keeps proving itself over and over: guys give love to get sex, and gals give sex to get love. The women never receive the love they want, but they get a whole lot more they don't want, when it's far too late to undo the trade. The guys get what they think they want, lose respect for the woman who gave it up to them, and move on to the next conquest.

However, women have far more power than they know to help men overcome their reluctance to marry.

What if most of the women in the U.S. said *no* to sex outside of marriage? Nearly *half of all men* in the NMP study said they would not marry a woman unless she agreed to live with them first. What if women just said *no* to living with their boyfriends? Think of the effect this would have on marriage rates: if the NMP issued a report in the year 2050 studying mating and marrying behavior in the first four decades of the twenty-first century in an America truly blessed by God, we would be celebrating a staggering turnaround in the trends.

HUNDRED-HUNDRED MARRIAGE

Statistics show that in the last four decades of the twentieth century, the percentage of women in the workforce steadily increased while the percentage of men declined. In 1960, the US workforce comprised 80 percent of the male population (age 16 and over) to 36 percent of the female population; in 2000, the ratio had changed to 71 percent of men and 58 percent of women.[40] Along with this trend came changing opinions about marriage roles, fueled by the influence of the women's movement. Television shows reflected the changing views, from the 1950s passive, intellectually challenged home ornament June Cleaver (*Leave It to Beaver*) to the 1980s power-wife Clair Huxtable (*The Cosby Show*), a career woman who had it all—partner in a law firm, happily married, loving but firm mother, equal in every way to her husband Cliff.

During this period of rapid social change, debates littered the landscape about who should be responsible for what in the marriage partnership. What was fair about working women continuing to bear responsibility for all the housework even though they were no longer at home for most of the day? Shouldn't fathers take on a more active role with children on a daily basis, to help ease the pressure on working moms?

In the 1970s especially, it wasn't unusual to hear of couples drawing up contracts to divide household and parenting responsibilities as evenly as possible down the middle: one cooked while the other did the dishes; one fed the kids breakfast and supervised school lunches while the other coordinated after-school carpools to sports practice and music lessons; laundry chores were redistributed so it was every man, woman, and child for himself or herself. The "equality" issue was taken so far that some couples applied it to such miniscule tasks as making the bed—"you make your side; I'll make mine."

In theory, the principle of shouldering household responsibilities equally is a fine idea. In practice, it can lead to keeping score and sniping at your spouse for not holding up his or her end. Someone once asked me, "Don't you think marriage is a fifty-fifty proposition?" And I said, "No, I think it is a hundred-hundred deal." You should go into marriage committed 100 percent to seeking your partner's happiness. Your partner should go into marriage committed 100 percent to seeking your happiness. And you should both enter marriage committed 100 percent to seeking the Lord's will.

So many people think, *I'm not happy in my marriage. He might as well be living on another planet. No matter how much I do, she always blames me for our problems. I deserve to be happy, and there's no future for me in this marriage. I'm getting out.* You know what that is? That's 100–zero marriage: my happiness matters 100 percent; my commitment to my spouse for better or for worse matters zero percent.

This is where the most disruption is taking place in our culture. Let's face it: why are 55 percent of our children spending a significant portion of their childhood and adolescence being reared in single-parent families? Because people are having sex outside marriage. Because husbands and wives are leaving their spouses, the mothers and fathers of their children, and taking up with a new partner chasing the carrot of "my happiness."

BLESSINGS THAT MIGHT RAIN DOWN

Marriage reduces the risk that adults will be either perpetrators or victims of crime. Men who are married to the women they are living with are far less likely to be physically violent toward them. Overall, single and divorced women are four to five times more likely to be victims of violent crime than married women. Single and divorced women are almost ten times more likely than wives to be raped. Unmarried men are about four times as likely as married men to become victims of violent crimes because they go a lot of places that married men don't go where they engage in riskier behavior.

Studies of chronic juvenile offenders have established that those who marry after reaching adulthood and stay married reduce their risk of repeat offenses by two-thirds, compared to offenders who do not marry or do not establish good marriages.

The one thing that would lift more people out of poverty than any other single factor is for women to be married—and stay married—to the father of their children. Divorce would shrink to a rare phenomenon. The vast majority of American children would once again be reared in intact families.

These are staggering factors.[41] Imagine the blessings that would pour forth upon our land *simply by improving marriage rates*. The America that God will bless is *not* out of our reach. It starts with a truly biblical sexuality. It grows with a truly biblical understanding and practice of marriage and family—so that husbands really do love their wives as Christ loves the church and gives Himself in sacrifice for it, and wives really do put themselves under the authority of their own husbands as unto the Lord.

Think of how this reality would change the views of the next generation about marriage. Think of how this reality would change behavior in dating and serious relationships. Let us envision an America in which divorce is rare: in which people get married, stay married, and children are reared in two-parent homes by their own mothers and fathers.

We know that on average, married couples build more wealth than single persons or cohabiting couples. Marriage partners appear to build more wealth for some of the same reasons that partnerships do in general: economically, they are more efficient. Marital social norms encourage healthy productive behavior and wealth accumulation. Married men earn more money than do single men with similar education and job history. Why? We don't know for certain, but married men appear to have greater work commitment, longer periods of employment, greater personal health, and more stable personal routines—including sleep, diet, and alcohol consumption. They also benefit from both the work effort and the emotional support they receive from their wives.

One autumn my wife and I traveled to an event in another state. I had a persistent cough, to which I was responding with typical manliness: do nothing and hope it goes away. My wife said, "Honey, when we get back home, you need to go see the doctor."

I said, "Dear, I don't have a fever; I only have a cough."

"You've been coughing far too long," she answered, "and you need to go see the doctor."

"Well, I don't have a fever," I replied, "and I don't have any rattle in my chest. And when I get home, I have to get on another plane and go speak at the evangelism conference to which I am committed."

My wife said, "Please go see the doctor."

So I went to see the doctor.

"You've got pneumonia," the doctor said. "If you had waited twenty-four hours longer, I would be admitting you to the hospital."

This is one reason why married men live ten years longer than single men. Their wives provide emotional and other means of support. In other words, they are persistent in reminding them to go to the doctor and get their checkups. They fuss at them when they don't eat right and take their vitamins. They protest when their husbands spend too much of their lives working and too little of their lives resting and enjoying their families.

Forty-year-old men who come from homes in which their parents divorced are three times more likely to die earlier than forty-year-old men who come from homes in which their parents stayed married. It appears that parental divorce sets off a negative chain of events, which contributes to a higher mortality risk later in life, especially among men.

Think about the economic impact of men living nearly ten years longer and enjoying greater health and well-being. For starters, health care insurance and costs would go way down. But crime rates would go down, too. Most women can function pretty well without men, but men tend to function poorly without women. Most of the violent antisocial behavior in our culture is perpetrated by men who are not living with their mothers or their wives. They live unchecked by the natural domesticating influence of women.

What if this trend were reversed, so that most men were living with female family members? Parental marriage is associated with a sharply lower risk of infant mortality. It is associated with significantly reduced rates of alcohol and substance abuse for both adults and teens. What these factors boil down to is this: if you want to fight the war on drugs, get married and stay married. Drug pushers would be out looking for work because they wouldn't have anyone to sell drugs to.

Married people have longer life expectancies, even after controlling for race, income, and family background. In most developed countries, middle-aged, single, divorced, or widowed men are about twice as likely to die in any given year as married men, and non-married women face a risk of death about one and one-half times greater than what married women face.

Marriage is also associated with lower rates of injury, illness, and disability for both men and women. Think about the impact on national health care costs if most people stayed married and retained good health into old age.

Naysayers are bound to protest, "It's naïve to think that just by eliminating divorce as a significant factor, it would solve our culture's problems." True, it would not solve everything, but just because it's not a panacea doesn't mean it wouldn't be a good place to start.

It stretches the imagination to conceive of what the average American community would look like if the overwhelming norm were stable homes with most children reared in them. Compared to what we are living with today, it's almost beyond imagination.

I'm old enough to remember, dimly, what American society looked like before the sexual revolution of the 1960s radically reconfigured it. Back then, there were a lot of stable marriages, but one of the problems was that there were a lot of unhappy women in those stable marriages. The culture was extremely chauvinistic in reducing women to simplistic roles. In many cases, husbands had no clue that their wives were unhappy, because it was presumed that all husbands needed to do was bring home the bacon and occasionally put the hammer down on disciplining the kids. This cultural stereotype was demeaning to both sexes, but it was especially demeaning to women.

I am not calling for a return to the 1950s. The America that God will bless is not an America of the past, but an America that has never been. I want us to imagine a future in which God pours out His blessing upon America in a way He has never done before. If enough Christians in this country committed themselves to repentance and righteousness to trigger a divine tipping point, God's blessings could heal our epidemic of divorce. Can you understand the social revolution this would unleash in America?

In this chapter we have looked at only the tip of the iceberg. In the next chapter, we will peer down into the depths of change that such a revolution would produce in the lives of our children.

﹐ 6 ﹐

Imagine! If we made sure that in America . . .

CHILDREN ARE NOT VICTIMIZED BY ADULTS

How does our country view its children? It would seem that in the land of the free and the home of the brave, victimization of children starts early in life.

In January 2004, the Partial-Birth Abortion Ban Act of 2003 was under review in federal court. The U.S. Department of Justice had commissioned the testimony of the highly distinguished Dr. Kanwaljeet Anand, a world-renowned physician and researcher specializing in pediatric critical care and the neurobiology of pain. Dr. Anand's pioneering work had already triggered significant change in the treatment of premature and newborn babies, when doctors began using pain medication for infants in surgery based on Anand's research published in 1987.[42]

In his January 2004 report for the court review, Dr. Anand presented detailed information on fetal development supporting his conviction that unborn babies are vulnerable to excruciating pain from the partial-birth abortion procedure:

It is my opinion that the human fetus possesses the ability to experience pain from 20 weeks of gestation, if not earlier, and the pain perceived by a fetus is possibly more intense than that perceived by term newborns or older children. The process of (a) grasping the lower extremity of a fetus with forceps or other surgical instrument, (b) manipulating or rotating the fetal position within the uterus, (c) forcible extraction of the fetal legs or lower body through the uterine cervix, (d) surgical incision of the fetal cranium/upper neck area of the fetus, and (e) entrance into the cranial vault (followed by vacuum suctioning of the fetal brain) during an abortion procedure will result in prolonged and intense pain experienced by the human fetus, if that fetus is at or beyond the neurological maturity associated with 20 weeks of gestation. Anesthetic agents that are routinely administered to the mother during this procedure would be insufficient to ensure that the fetus does not feel pain, and the higher doses of anesthetic drugs, enough to produce fetal anesthesia, would seriously compromise the health of the mother. Thus, it is my opinion that the fetus would be

subjected to intense pain, occurring prior to fetal
demise, from the abortion procedures described in
the Partial-Birth Abortion Ban Act of 2003.[43]

Ron Fitzsimmons, executive director of the National Coalition
of Abortion Providers, provoked outrage when he admitted on a
televised *Nightline* segment (26 February 1997) that he had delib-
erately under-reported the number of partial-birth abortions performed each year as 450 while testifying in government hearings.
The actual figure, he said, was between three thousand and four
thousand each year.

The Partial-Birth Abortion Ban Act of 2003 required doctors to
inform women of the medical evidence that unborn babies feel
pain in the life-ending procedure used in pregnancies of five
months or longer. Dr. Anand's medical opinion ran counter to
claims from abortion-rights activists that the anesthesia provided
to the mother during the abortion was sufficient to medicate any
pain experienced by the unborn child. The ban would require
doctors to offer women the use of anesthesia for the unborn child,
although Dr. Anand testified that the amount of anesthesia
required to relieve the pain of the child would put the mother's life
at risk.

Obviously, the crux of the matter starts way before the third
trimester: before conception, with two individuals' moral choices
regarding their sexuality; at conception, with their respect or
disrespect for the unique and inherent value of every human life.
But when it comes down to individual lifestyle choices, children
have no business interfering with the rights of adults in this arena,
it would seem, and they suffer the consequences.

A society that fails to recognize life as a gift from a divine Creator can manipulate the definition of "life" in order to justify its behavior—and therefore champion the personal gratification of self-centered human beings even when it is built on abuse of other human beings. Those in power do the victimizing, and they pick the weak and helpless—or render them weak and helpless—because they have no power to fight back.

Abortion at any stage ends the life of an innocent human being. We don't draw and quarter the worst criminals any more, and yet we subject the youngest and most innocent among us to the equivalent of that horrific death and worse. The very least that any civilized people can do is minimize the pain and suffering of the smallest and most defenseless human beings among them as their lives are being violently stolen.

Yet in June 2004, federal judge Phyllis Hamilton ruled that a ban on partial-birth abortions imposes an "undue burden" on a woman's right to an abortion during the second trimester of pregnancy. The moral compass of our federal judiciary has been grossly demagnetized. It continues to go haywire under pressure from groups such as Planned Parenthood, which hailed Judge Hamilton's decision as a victory for women's rights over against the ideological agenda of antichoice extremists.

How could we have allowed our moral standards to sink so low that we would be having a national debate on whether it's right or wrong to kill an unborn baby during induced delivery by puncturing its skull? Our society has already granted legal protection to unborn children in acts of physical violence against pregnant women by criminal assailants, yet it grants legal protection to doctors who perform acts of violence against women and their unborn children through a barbarous and horrific act solely intended to result in the gruesome death of the baby.

But then we live in a time when abortion is one of the most common surgical procedures in the U.S. According to a report jointly issued in January 2003 by the Alan Guttmacher Institute and Physicians for Reproductive Choice and Health, 1,310,000 abortions (90 percent in the first trimester) were performed in the U.S. in the year 2000 alone. The primary reasons for these abortions were all related to how disruptive it would be to have a baby: financial difficulties, unprepared for the responsibility, too much change, relationship with the father not strong enough, mother too young and immature.

In the interests of self-gratification—more money, an easier life, sexual freedom without responsibility, a form of intimacy without commitment—we victimize children before they are even out of the womb.

Loving parents who bond with their children will stop at nothing to keep them out of harm's way, protect them from imminent danger, and rescue them from crisis. Yet the evidence of how America raises her children looks like anything but such loving care. Consider a few statistics from the Child Welfare League of America:[44]

- Children in America are more likely to live in poverty than any other age group.
- The rate of child neglect is more than one out of every two children. Over two of every ten children are physically abused, and more than one in ten children are sexually abused. Children under three are most likely to be abused and neglected.

- Children between six and eleven years old are much more likely to commit violent acts when they live in homes with substance abuse in the family, low socioeconomic status, and aggression.
- Between 1.5 million and 3.3 million children witness some form of violence in the home each year.
- Children from violent homes exhibit more aggressive and delinquent behavior compared with children from non-violent homes.
- Between 50 percent and 70 percent of men who abuse their female partners also abuse their children.
- Children constitute over one-quarter of the homeless population in America.
- According to the U.S. Department of Health and Human Services, 75 to 80 percent of children who need mental health services do not receive them.
- Children whose parents abuse drugs and alcohol are almost three times more likely to be abused and four times more likely to be neglected than are children of parents who are not substance abusers.
- Four million children, ages thirteen to fourteen, spend time unsupervised on a regular basis.
- Most violence against juveniles occurs during the hours of 3:00 p.m. through 7:00 p.m.
- The leading cause of death for youth ages fifteen through twenty-four is homicide.

Why are children in America in such grave trouble?

Before we plunge into the problems, I want to say a word to those of you who may be single parents—unwed or divorced—or remarried and negotiating a blended family. We are going to be looking at some sobering statistics, and you may at first feel discouraged. You might think, *Dr. Land, thanks for the bad news, but I can't go back and redo the past. I didn't want this to happen any more than you did. Do you have to rub salt in my family wounds?*

Please know, first, that it is neither my place nor my purpose to judge you. Nor do I want to discourage you. In fact, I hope that if you recognize your family circumstances in any of these at-risk scenarios, you will seek a supportive safety network in the body of Christ, at a local church God provides for you where the gospel is preached and the authority of the Word of God is upheld. I am not a stranger to broken-family pain, and I pray you and your children will experience healing—and restoration of the years the locusts have eaten (see Joel 2:24–26).

However, if we who are called by God's name are going to humble ourselves together, and pray, and seek the Lord's face, then we need to repent, and that means acknowledging the many ways in which we have fallen short of the glory of God. Every one of us is a fallen human being in need of the Savior's redemption. If we are going to seek healing for our land, we must be honest in naming our national wounds. Only you and God and those to whom He has placed you in accountability know what specific shortcomings you may need to bring before the Lord.

Remember the good news that if you will confess your sins, then God is faithful and just to forgive your sins *and to cleanse you from all unrighteousness* (see 1 John 1:9). You can move forward, freed from guilt, to do what is right before the Lord and to love your children in the power of Christ's love and in the knowledge of His wisdom. God bless you, and God bless your precious children.

So I ask you, therefore, to stay with me as we move through this difficult material—not to dwell on what is wrong, but to envision how much can be made right in the divine providence of God.

VICTIMS OF DIVORCE

In the previous chapter we explored the damaging consequences on marriage of a culture that refuses to bend the knee to anyone or anything other than its own idols. Divorce has become so common that we have been lulled into thinking it's normal for kids to split their time between multiple residences, to experience their mom and dad separately with different partners instead of together in the home, and to negotiate the challenges of a blended family.

Duke University has published a study across twenty-seven years that followed the effects of divorce on children.[45] Its findings are some of the most devastating evidence I've seen. Children whose parents divorced have higher rates of physiological distress and mental illness. In fact, divorce appears to increase the risk of suicide significantly. Boys raised in single-parent families are far more likely to engage in delinquent and criminal behavior.

Growing up outside an intact marriage increases the likelihood that children will grow up and raise the next generation outside an intact marriage. Children with unwed parents are more likely to become unwed parents. Children of divorced parents are more likely to end a marriage in divorce. Children reared outside intact marriages are more likely to become sexually active, at earlier ages, with a future of unhappy relationships and broken marriages.

Surprisingly, divorce is most likely to be transmitted across generations when parents in relatively low-conflict marriages divorced.

Think about that. In other words, it's *less* likely that divorce will be perpetuated in the next generation if the marriage broke up over explosive situations such as a physically abusive or promiscuous spouse, or the prevalence of substance abuse. When the divorce occurs with much lower thresholds of conflict, it is more likely that the children will themselves divorce in the future.

Divorce and unmarried child-bearing greatly increases poverty for both children and mothers. This is one strong argument for the move to eliminate the marriage tax and increase incentives for married couples. *The single most important factor that could have the greatest effect in helping to resolve poverty in the United States is if women would marry the fathers of their children.* This one change would provide more immediate and dramatic relief than anything else we could do. That's because the single greatest cause of poverty in this country is out-of-wedlock and single-parent families.

Research also shows that children's health is adversely affected by divorce. Dr. Deborah Dawson of Case Western Reserve University has found that children from broken homes are at higher risk for headaches, asthma, speech defects, and injury; and children living with single mothers are also more likely than children from two-parent homes to receive help from professionals for emotional problems.[46]

Parental divorce or failure to marry increases children's risk of school failure. Children of divorced or unwed parents have lower grades among other measures of academic achievement. They are more likely to be held back, more likely to drop out of high school, less likely to graduate from college and find well-paying jobs. Even after controlling for race and family background, *children whose parents divorce end up with significantly lower levels of education than children in single-mother families created by the death of the father.*

Now that's a powerful statement. What matters most is not the absence of the father as much as it is *why* the father left. Children whose parents remarry do no better on average than children who live with single mothers. It's the divorce that causes the harm.

The research is undeniably, unequivocally clear that the welfare of children is improved in all respects when they are reared in the traditional family structure. As Princeton sociologists Sara McLanahan and Gary Sandefur observed, "If we were asked to design a system for making sure that children's basic needs were met, we would probably come up with something quite similar to the two-parent ideal."[47]

Victims of Fatherlessness

Fatherlessness is epidemic in our society, thanks in large part to the simple physiological fact that women bear children. It is much easier for a father to walk away from his parental responsibilities—if he is even aware of them.

We know from observation and scientific analysis that a father has more to do with the formation of the sexuality of both daughters and sons than does the mother. It has been substantially proven now that one of the critical roles a father plays is helping son and daughter establish their sexuality in normative and healthy ways.

A girl who loses her father in the home before her sixth birthday is *five times* as likely to become sexually active before her sixteenth birthday as a girl whose father is in the home through her sixth birthday. Now we could spend a lot of time talking about the devastating consequences of that statistic, and what would happen if that were not the case. But I think we would all agree—even liberals, unless they're just pagans—that girls younger than sixteen being sexually active is catastrophic from any perspective: emotionally, psychologically, physiologically, relationally.

A boy who loses his father from the home is *three hundred times* more likely to get in trouble with the law between the ages of twelve and twenty-two. This factor is the single biggest predictor of juvenile delinquency—more so than a boy's intelligence, education, religion, or socioeconomic status. If his mother remarries after the divorce, that doesn't help because the emotional dynamic is not that he gains a father, but that he loses his mother because her primary focus shifts from her son to her new husband.

In the absence of a father's role in discipline, single mothers report more conflict with and less monitoring of their children. Young adults whose parents are divorced are twice as likely to report poor relationships with their mothers as young adults whose parents remained married. The cost to relationships with fathers is even worse. One national study found that 29 percent of children from nondivorced families reported a poor relationship with their father, compared to 65 percent of children from divorced homes. In most cases, social dynamics alone contribute to this, because children see divorced fathers less frequently and generally have less affectionate relationships with their fathers.

Even when biological but unmarried fathers remain in the home, the relationship is still less affectionate because cohabitation is not the functional equivalent of marriage. In other words, the dynamics are very different.

Discerning how to meet the needs of children in this culture requires that we face the challenges honestly: it's just not possible for a single parent—no matter how good a job he or she is trying to do alone—to provide everything that two healthy parents in a healthy marriage can for nurturing the emotional, spiritual, and neurophysiological development of children.

Dr. Ed Young, pastor of the approximately forty-thousand-member Second Baptist Church in Houston, Texas, is author of *The Ten Commandments of Marriage.*[48] Young has three grown sons, all in full-time ministry, and eight grandchildren—seven of whom are girls. I was privileged to interview him as a guest on our *For Faith & Family* radio program. Our conversation turned to the idea fostered in American society that fathers are optional in rearing children.

"Children without fathers face so many areas in life where they will be unable to relate," Young said. "Girls will have trouble relating to the opposite sex. Boys will have difficulty learning to be a man because they haven't grown up with a father to role model for them. This is why it is so important for single parents to have other adults in their children's lives to help provide surrogate role models, picking up some of the deficit of the missing parent."

"Richard, I know you give your daughters and your son physical affection," he went on. "That's so important for both genders: if you have a daughter, kiss and hug her. If you have a son, kiss and hug him. Give your kids emotional support as well as being there physically for them, and when they're grown with kids of their own they will have an example to follow in their family. And if you really want to know how to give your children love, spell it T-I-M-E. Next to your relationship with the Lord and your marriage, give your highest priority to *being with* your children. When my boys were growing up I said if they all turn out to be thugs it's because they spent so much time with their daddy."[49]

VICTIMS OF PORNOGRAPHY

News accounts are filled with horrific stories of child-on-child violence. In one incident, a little girl was stalked in a casino and raped and strangled in a restroom. The fifteen-year-old boy who confessed to the crime had a whole closet full of violent child pornography that he had downloaded off the Internet. His parents had no clue. When interviewed, all they said was that they noticed their son had been spending a lot of time in his room and had seemed to become more remote and withdrawn recently.

Hello? Anybody home?

The porn predator is stalking and destroying our nation's children. We know from extensive research, including the *Attorney General's Report on Pornography,* that child molesters cite child pornography as the single greatest weapon in their arsenal, because they use it to seduce children. They show children pictures of adults and children engaged in sexual activity and say, "Look, these people are doing it, so it's okay for us to do it." Then they victimize and seduce these children. Volumes of sadomasochistic homosexual pornography were taken from serial killer and pedophile Jeffrey Dahmer's apartment when he was captured.

Sexual violence against women and children has gone up exponentially in this culture. It will accelerate at unprecedented levels as boys at earlier and earlier ages are exposed to hard-core pornography on the Internet. The average age used to be fourteen;

now it's eight. Imagine what exposure to that filth does to an eight, nine-, or ten-year-old boy.

When it comes down to individual lifestyle choices, children have no business interfering with the rights of adults in this arena, it would seem. In 1996, in an attempt to stanch the swollen tide, Congress passed the Communications Decency Act, prohibiting online computer distribution of obscene and indecent material to children under eighteen. The following year, the CDA was struck down by the Supreme Court, which ruled that it violated the First Amendment.

The year after that, 1998, Congress responded by passing a more specifically targeted law barring Web sites from making sexually explicit material available for commercial purposes to children under seventeen. The Child Online Protection Act was challenged in federal court, which issued a preliminary injunction banning its enforcement. When the case went before the U.S. Supreme Court in June 2004, the high court upheld the injunction against COPA, ruling that it was a burden on some constitutionally protected free speech and that it was unnecessary because less restrictive means of protecting minors, such as filtering software, already existed.

The Supreme Court still doesn't get it—but it is a step behind Congress, the president, and thousands of parents in America who do. It is the responsibility of society—including the government—to protect children from exposure to this emotional and spiritual toxic waste called online pornography. Because the court continues to reflect a society more preoccupied with so-called "adult rights" than adult obligations to protect children, parents must do even more to protect their children against this spiritual terrorist assault on their homes—while insisting that government shoulder its responsibility as well.

What Children Need

Imagining an America blessed by God can involve quite a stretch of the imagination—except when society itself discovers that our most critical needs point to solutions that just so happen to be aligned with Judeo-Christian truth. One of the most striking examples of this convergence made headline news in September 2003 with the publication of a Report to the Nation from the Commission on Children at Risk, entitled *Hardwired to Connect: The New Scientific Case for Authoritative Communities.*

The Commission warned that one in five children in America are at serious risk for emotional and physiological problems because of a "connection crisis." Its report presented extensive scientific evidence that the human brain is hard-wired for two fundamental kinds of connection: horizontally, in close relationships with other human beings; and vertically, in finding moral and spiritual meaning through a relationship with a transcendent divine being.

For example, science has established a biological basis for the intensified search for meaning that occurs in adolescence. In other words, young people's involvement in religious activities is not a product of social conditioning, but a deep-seated drive in their physiological make-up. In turn, portions of the brain that undergo significant development in adolescence are activated by religious experience.

This means not only that it is vital to provide children with stable, close relationships with family and community, and to nurture their need for moral and spiritual meaning, but that failure to do so actually inhibits their biological development and keeps them from flourishing. When more than half our children are spending all or part of their childhood and adolescence in single-parent families, we are diminishing the environment that directly affects their neurological development—and therefore their future capacity to establish close interpersonal relationships and to focus on an ultimate transcendent relationship that fulfills their deepest needs for understanding meaning and purpose.

In other words, we have been practicing collective emotional, spiritual, and physiological abuse on an entire generation of our children!

The Report summarizes ten primary conclusions from scientific research as evidence of our biologically based connection needs:

1. *The human brain organizes itself in a relational context (i.e. with another person) that is either growth-facilitating or growth-inhibiting.* Children's ability to regulate their emotions and behaviors is either strengthened or weakened by this relational context, meaning that later on they will either be defended against or vulnerable to forming psychiatric disorders. In addition, attachment hormones involved in parent-infant bonding appear to be the same ones associated later in life with relationship intimacy. We know that relational intimacy among adults boosts immune systems and increases healing rates for physical wounds.

2. *Parental nurturing is transmitted to future generations not just by social modeling, but also by genetic means.* Offspring of nurturing mothers carry that same nurturing capacity in their genes. Even into adolescence, parental presence appears to affect children

biologically. For example, researchers have discovered that the onset of puberty in girls is slowed by living in close proximity to the biological father, and accelerated by living with a biologically unrelated male such as a stepfather or mother's boyfriend.

3. *The nature-vs-nurture debate is obsolete, because we now know that social environments change genetic material in children.* Good parenting and weak parenting is passed to future generations in our DNA. However, an improved social environment can actually offset—genetically—the inheritance of weak parenting. The cycle of family violence can be broken at the physiological level.

4. *The adolescent brain is wired for risk-taking and novelty-seeking.* When children reach the teen years and begin the process of separating from parents, they are particularly vulnerable to the consequences of experimentation. Substance abuse affects their developing brains more harshly than those of adults. The absence of a nurturing environment in which their biological impulses can be guided and constructively channeled leaves teens dependent on peers for such support, often with disastrous consequences. The good news is that a nurturing environment has a positive effect on the actual neurocircuitry of the teenage brain. Parents rarely witness this cause-and-effect, of course—but if you are parenting a teen, remind yourself of it the next time you tangle over boundaries!

5. *The need to attach social significance and personal meaning to gender is a deep, universal human need.* When toddlers develop body awareness, they depend on relationship with the same-sex-as-me and opposite-sex-as-me parents. The gender identity that begins to develop at this age is a physiological, familial, and psychosocial process that deeply influences individuals throughout

their entire lives. Teens in particular need a positive environment that gives them a context for understanding and expressing their maturing sexuality. Our society's widespread attempts to deconstruct and devalue gender, largely in response to the agenda of homosexual activists, has pulled the rug out from under our teens. They are left with peer pressure and a highly sexualized culture for understanding their gender identity and establishing rites of passage through puberty. The Commission diplomatically observed that important issues are bound up in social concerns about gender, but they warned that responding to such concerns by abdicating responsibility for the gender needs of adolescents is a dangerous neglect.

6. *Our moral sense originates in our attachment wiring. Close attachments in infancy yield healthy moral development later on; impoverished attachments in infancy erode moral understanding of right and wrong, love and hurt, honesty and deceit.* Our biologically bas ed need for attachment—for feeling loved and protected and understood—is so important that it has a biological effect on what our moral worldview is as adults.

7. *As moral development continues into adulthood and attachment needs expand beyond family to other relationships and social groups, community becomes critically important in helping individuals find meaning beyond self-centered pursuits.* Our hard-wiring for moral and spiritual connection continues throughout our lives. Positive social role models, for example, have a direct effect on the development of positive social behavior—and the reverse is true as well. A society that neglects its responsibility to inculcate moral identity can expect moral chaos.

8. *Horizontal connectedness through primary relationships and vertical connectedness through spiritual experience have the same kinds of influence on our biological development of attachment needs.* Children tend to attribute to God traits exhibited in their parents, and so early family development can exert a lifelong influence on spiritual development, positively or negatively. However, spiritual connectedness has been shown to have the same nurturing effect as primary relationships in setting a course for long-term survival and relational skills.

9. *Religiosity and spirituality positively affect well-being across many categories of life—but for teens, the positive effects of personal devotion are twice as strong as for adults.* Science has now moved far beyond "prayer works" in its findings of how spiritual and religious experiences improve our lives. What is particularly surprising in the Report is to hear that we are hard-wired from our very infancy, at a level as basic as our primary need for the love of a mother and father, to find a close connection with God. In fact, the Commission suggested that the search for a spiritual relationship with a divine Creator is wired into an adolescent's developmental process.

10. *The human brain is wired to ask ultimate questions and seek ultimate answers.* This aspect of our make-up is such a deep-seated drive that we should no longer call it "religious," according to the Report, because it is fundamental to being human. Remember, this opinion is based not on the opinions of religious people claiming that everyone should be religious; it is based on evidence from scientific research and developments in our understanding of the human brain. If we are not providing a way for children to develop

a relationship with God, we are depriving them of something they need *at a biological level.*[50]

The Commission observed that in recent decades, the weakening of social institutions in the U.S. that foster these two kinds of connectedness has led to our current crisis of neglected children and adolescents. The solution lies in what they call "authoritative communities," which balance warmth and structure in an environment created and sustained to allow children to flourish. Simply defined, authoritative communities are groups of people who are committed to modeling and transmitting the connections that children need for healthy growth and development—in other words, to passing along to the next generation what it means to be a good person and to live a good life. The emphasis in recent decades on treating children with drugs has had some helpful—if debatable—effects in treating symptoms, observed the Commission , but it leaves the root problem unaddressed.

Authoritative communities reflect the positive benefits of authoritative parenting—close emotional connections but firmness in setting expectations and establishing guidelines. This kind of parenting has been shown most effective for positive psychological and emotional development in children. Characteristics of authoritative communities will come as no surprise to those who are raising their children in a Christian family and connecting them with a significant church community. The "Hardwired to Connect" report has identified these ten criteria for the kinds of communities we desperately need:

1. a social institution that includes children and youth;
2. children are treated as ends in themselves, not means to an end;

3. warm and nurturing;

4. expectations and limits are clearly established;

5. core membership comprises caring and involved adults, not hired professionals;

6. multigenerational;

7. long-term;

8. shared understanding of what it means to be a good person;

9. fosters spiritual and religious development; and

10. treats all people as valuable and is based on the principle of loving your neighbor.

Striking a Healthy Family Balance

Neglect of children occurs not only in environments of poverty and abuse and abandonment, but also in the middle of socioeconomic comfort. Notice the emphasis on boundaries, guidelines, expectations, and consequences in the "Hardwired to Connect" report. Children are also neglected and deprived in the absence of such a structure. And in a society dedicated to personal gratification and the pursuit of "the good life," many parents find it easier to abdicate their responsibilities. They may try to bribe their children's cooperation with material things. They may depend on computers, video games, and television to keep their children occupied. Many parents leave older children unsupervised—and unparented. Type A parents substitute activities and achievement opportunities for involvement with their children, keeping their kids so busy with extracurricular activities there is no time for quality family interaction.

This kind of neglect has led to what Ed Young, Jr. calls "Kid CEO"—a household in which the children are in charge, either directly or indirectly. This Ed Young is the son of Dr. Ed Young, author of *The Ten Commandments of Marriage*. Ed Jr., senior pastor of Fellowship Church in Grapevine, Texas (one of the fastest-growing churches in our country), wrote *Kid CEO: How to Keep Children from Running Your Life* for families enmeshed in power struggles: "Many parents are losing ground," he writes. "Homes that look great on the outside, with beautiful architecture, white picket fences, and immaculate lawns, on the inside are packed with confusion, conflict, and chaos. Parents, let's face it: there is a crisis buried deep within the family. . . . What is happening in these homes is a crisis of leadership."[51] A Parent CEO family, he maintains, is modeled on God's design for the family and is characterized first and foremost by the parents' commitment to their relationship with God first, to their marriage second, and to the kids third. Only when the power hierarchy is properly established can parents provide the loving and nurturing environment their children need—while simultaneously nurturing a healthy marriage.

IMAGINE ALL THE CHILDREN SAFE AND WELL

When we reach a place in which God is pouring out His blessings on America, it will happen because we have reached a divine tipping point: a divinely ordained critical mass of people who are called by His name, who have humbled themselves and prayed and sought His face and turned from their wicked ways.

What would America look like if virtually our entire citizenship believed that society must affirm the sacred worth of every human life, from beginning to end? What changes would we see in our culture and in the events of history if the values and mores and laws of our society were based on the obligation of the powerful to protect the weak and vulnerable?

Let us pray and work for that moment in our nation's history when partial-birth abortion is viewed as a great evil, the "Uncle Tom's Cabin" of the abortion movement. Just as Harriet Beecher Stowe's *Uncle Tom's Cabin* put a human face on the evil institution of slavery, making its continuance intolerable to the American people, so will partial-birth abortion put a human face on the evil of abortion, making abortion on demand intolerable to a majority of the American people.

Let us pray and work for that moment when the current 55 percent of children being reared in single-parent homes has been reduced to 2 percent . . . when our children flourish in nurturing primary relationships in families, in nurturing spiritual relationships in their family and church contexts, and in authoritative communities dedicated to providing the social structures our children need for physical, emotional, psychological, moral, and spiritual development.

Let us work and pray for the day when collectively we are teaching our children the significance—socially, morally, and spiritually—of being male and female . . . that they are equal to each other and they complement each other, but they are not interchangeable . . . that gender is a gift to be treated with respect and honor.

Let us commit ourselves to the elimination of so much of our societal child abuse that instead of 25 percent of our children failing to reach productive childhood, only 1 percent needs crisis care.

Let us seek to reestablish marriage as the overwhelming dominant norm in this culture, so that female promiscuity is drastically reduced because girls have good relationships with their fathers . . . so that sexually active teenagers are the rare exception, not the norm . . . so that children and teens understand their maturing sexuality from parents and positive role models, not from pornography . . . so that fathers stay married to the mothers of their children, reducing poverty and eliminating much of the antisocial and criminal behavior of boys.

Imagine all the children—safe and well, heaven above them and solid ground below them, loved by God and by their parents and by their neighbors. Imagine an America in which this has come true. It's not as far away as you might think.

، 7 ،

Imagine! If a significant portion of our population comprised . . .

CHRISTIANS WHO ARE RADICAL CHANGE AGENTS

Contemporary culture is home to two very disparate civilizations: the Judeo-Christian civilization, which is founded on belief in the sanctity of all human life, and the neopagan civilization, which is based on a personal-gratification, quality-of-life philosophy.

When these antagonistic worldviews come up against each other, the outcome makes a real difference in peoples' lives—

because real people die when the quality-of-life ethic usurps the sanctity-of-life ethic. And thirty years of *Roe v. Wade*—killing a baby every twenty seconds—has severely eroded the sanctity of human life ethic in the United States. We have brutalized our entire society, including our court system, by devaluing human life so severely that a court can as casually sentence a human being such as Terry Schiavo to die by malnutrition and dehydration as it can allow a partially delivered healthy baby to be murdered by a physician.

The only hope is for the people of God to stand up and say, "Enough is enough!" We stand at a critical juncture, and the choices we make will produce long-lasting results. In another fifteen years we will live in a different world than we do today. What kind of world will it be?

Take a Stand Against Pornography

When the Attorney General's Commission on Pornography released its Report in 1986, each Commission member contributed an individual statement providing his or her personal commentary on the findings of the Report and their implications. Commissioner Diane D. Cusack felt that the most important conclusion was the imperative that law enforcement officials "should start committing maximum resources to enforcing the law."[52]

However, Cusack observed, much of the pornography under examination was sexually explicit material that did not qualify as "obscene" under legal definitions. Therefore, she warned, material that qualifies as "protected speech" under the First Amendment still carries the threat of undermining "2500 years of western civilization" in which "human sexuality and its expressions have been cherished as a private act between a loving couple committed to each other. This has created the strongest unit of society—the family. If our families become less wholesome, weaker, and less committed to the fidelity that is their core, our entire society will weaken as well."[53]

Legal safeguards against pornography are important, but they are not enough to staunch the dangerous flow of materials that will "seriously undermine our social fabric," according to Cusack. "These materials, whose message is clearly that sexual pleasure and self-gratification are paramount, have the ability to seriously undermine our social fabric. It is the individuals in our great nation who must see this, and reverse the trend—not the government."[54]

Do you want to be a change agent? *Take a stand against pornography.* It has so permeated our culture that we no longer have any boundaries keeping it out of homes, schools, stores, libraries, popular entertainment, and the collective consciousness of our nation. It is one of the biggest industries in the country; it is addictive; it is a subterranean electronic river of pure evil oozing up through modems into potentially every home in America. The vilest and most disgusting material that until very recently was relegated to the back alleys of the worst parts of the worse cities in America is now available anywhere in the United States where there is electricity and people have access to the Internet.

It is one of the great hidden causes of divorce in this culture. It is promoting a satanic counterfeit of God's gift of gender and sexuality. It is in the process of destroying the minds of millions upon millions of men and boys who in turn are destroying the lives of millions of women and girls. We are creating a generation of sexual predators and destroying the ability of millions of men and boys to be the husbands and fathers that God created them to be by exposure to this spiritual and emotional toxic waste.

If four thousand babies a day are being killed through abortion, then more than four thousand human lives are being destroyed every day by exposure to pornography, addiction to pornography, and the acts of sexual violence that they perpetrate on their victims, who have been anesthetized, twisted, and distorted by exposure to Satan's counterfeit of human sexuality.

Pornography is one of the most powerful weapons in Satan's arsenal. He uses it to corrupt God's beautiful plans for us as sexual beings. Pornography encourages lust, which then enslaves us, for sexual desire is the second most powerful motivation human beings have after the survival instinct. Unfortunately, the Internet has given this perversion nearly unimaginable reach and power.

The Bible tells us, "Do not love the world or anything in the world. If anyone loves the world, the love of the Father is not in him. For everything in the world—the cravings of sinful man, the lust of his eyes and the boasting of what he has and does—comes not from the Father but from the world. The world and its desires pass away, but the man who does the will of God lives forever" (1 John 2:15–17).

Pornography is a medium of both mental and physical images. We must constantly remind ourselves that we live in a world distorted by sin and must be careful what we allow our eyes to see.

Unfortunately, one reason many people in our society have been so susceptible to pornography is that far too often in American churches, particularly in conservative churches, we have shied away from teaching the full biblical revelation about human sexuality.

We know all about the *don'ts*. We know that First Corinthians 6 says our bodies are not intended for sexual immorality. But too often evangelical Christians have failed to adequately understand the Song of Solomon and share its truths with our young people. If First Corinthians records the *don'ts*, the Song of Solomon records the *do's*. The Song of Solomon says that sex is holy and that God created us as sexual beings to bring about the most loving, caring, giving union that a man and woman can know this side of heaven. If you think God doesn't approve of sex, you need to read a good modern translation of the Song of Solomon. However, our culture has made sex "dirty" by selfish misapplication.

Hebrews 13:4 says the marriage bed should be kept pure and that marriage should be honored by all. If anyone needed to be told the appropriate place and purpose for sexual relations, it was the first-century Corinthians. Corinth was the cultural cesspool of the Roman Empire. The Romans had a word for someone who had been hopelessly debauched. They'd say, "Well, he has been Corinthianized." That's how bad it was in Corinth.

It was out of this degenerate society that the Corinthian Christians were saved. Paul admonished them in 1 Corinthians 6:18, "Flee from sexual immorality!" Every sin a person can commit is outside the body, but the person who is sexually immoral sins against his own body. Paul knew that God created us as sexual beings to make of two people one flesh, and that we cannot separate ourselves from our sexuality.

There is no such thing as casual sex, therefore, because Paul says a person who has been promiscuous in mind or body is profoundly changed. This flies in the face of those in the pornography industry who insist pornography is a private matter and doesn't affect anyone else. People who view pornography are changed in their view of women, their view of procreation, and their view of the world. And that means they affect you and me.

Pornography perverts and distorts all of the God-given purposes for sexual intimacy. Pornography teaches people to disregard the sanctity of marriage and the gift of knowing one person intimately within its confines. It teaches people to view sex as a form of recreation, without regard for the welfare of one's sexual partner. We are weak, fallible creatures and subject to temptation. I have heard Adrian Rogers offer the sage advice, "To avoid falling down, don't walk on slippery surfaces." Steer clear of temptation and see that your family does the same. Don't pick up that magazine or click that mouse if it will subject you to temptation. The Bible tells us to flee from such (2 Timothy 2:22).

Don't underestimate the lure of this sordid material. No person—Christian or not—is above temptation when it comes to pornography, particularly with its easy accessibility on-line. If you have Internet access on your home or office computer, make sure you have a reliable filter that screens out the so-called "adult" sites.

Otherwise, having the Internet is like ordering magazines about subjects that interest you, then having them delivered in a box that also contains pornographic magazines you didn't order and don't want. "Well," most Internet providers would say, "if you want a magazine about baseball or American history, you have to take delivery of these others too. You don't have to look at them, though." For the sake of yourself and your family, get a good filter or get off the Internet.

Another way families can seek protection from Internet pornography is by supporting legislation to control it. When a bill is introduced that will reduce the exposure of children—and everyone else—to pornography on the Internet, support the politicians who champion it. They are fighting against long odds, for the porn industry is powerful and will do all it can to keep the electronic river of slime flowing unimpeded. Let morally responsible leaders know you're behind them. Pray for them and for yourself. And pray that the victims of pornography will feel the presence of God in their hearts soon, climb out of that fetid river, and bask in His glory.

Dr. Park Dietz, a criminal psychiatrist with degrees in medicine, public health, and sociology, was a member of the Attorney General's Commission on Pornography. His personal statement accompanying the Report was one of the most powerful indictments of pornography—an impassioned plea to Americans:

> [If] we do not act with compassion and conviction and courage for the hostages and victims of the pornographers we do not deserve the freedoms that our founding fathers bequeathed us. It has been nearly two centuries since Phillipe Pinel struck the chains from the mentally ill and more than a century since Abraham Lincoln struck the chains from America's black slaves. With this statement I ask you, America, to strike the chains from America's women and children, to free them from the bonds of pornography, to free them from the bonds of sexual abuse, to free them from the bonds of inner torment that entrap the second-class citizen in an otherwise free nation.[55]

TAKE A STAND FOR COMMITMENT

Long-term relationships—with friends, family members, and in the lifetime commitment of marriage—are in trouble. In preceding chapters we have looked at many reasons for this crisis and many consequences as a result of this crisis.

At the root of all this conflict, I think, is the basic problem of pride. "I want to do it my way." We take that sin into our marriage relationships, and we have to deal with it. For those in a difficult marriage, this might start with looking at why they got into that marriage in the first place, and how they can break the cycle of sin that encumbered that marriage with the personal baggage that each person carried into it.

This gets into family systems therapy—the exploration of how we are influenced by the way our family "system" operated. Families are not collections of individuals acting independently of one another; they are mini-communities of interdependent people who learn roles and behaviors and acquire expectations and obligations that take on life-and-death importance. Our family determines who we are and how we enter the world, and it is our first and last line of natural defense against the threats and dangers of the world. It is also our primary learning laboratory for how to go out into that world on our own and succeed in it.

For example, we can see family system dynamics in the lives of Franklin Delano and Eleanor Roosevelt. FDR's father was a good thirty years older than FDR's mother, and the two had a remote relationship. As a result, Franklin's mother over-invested herself in Franklin, trying to experience with her son some of the emotional intimacy and sense of being needed that she was not getting from her husband. Franklin's enmeshed relationship with his mother made it difficult for him to form a healthy emotional attachment to another female.

Eleanor lost her father when she was a very young girl, so she had an overly invested relationship with her mother, which made it difficult for her to form a healthy relationship with a male. When Franklin and Eleanor, who were second cousins, married each other, at first they seemed an ideal pair.

She didn't want a close bond with a man, and he didn't want a close bond with a woman. Franklin's mother came to live with them, taking the place of the matriarch at the family table, driving the relationship further apart. The White House was not a happy place, and the couple led separate lives.

What many people outside Christian faith say is that you can't overcome the patterns you inherit from your family of origin—your background is your destiny. If it is a negative background, you are doomed. But Christianity says, this explains it, but you're not doomed by it. You can overcome it—even after you've gotten married and enmeshed in one another's dynamics. If you and your spouse are ready to work on it, you can overcome it.

Background, environment, and circumstances are not destiny. You can't change the past, but you can change the impact the past has had on you. Sometimes you can't change the circumstances of the present—but you can change the person who is facing those circumstances. Paul prayed for the Lord to take away the thorn in his flesh, but instead of taking it away, the Lord gave him the strength to endure it. "My grace is sufficient for you, for my power is made perfect in weakness," the Lord told him (2 Corinthians 12:9).

Do you want to be a change agent? If you are married, then *take a stand for lifelong commitment to your spouse.*

"Marriage is the greatest theological school God has ever designed," says Dr. Ed Young, author of *The Ten Commandments of Marriage.*[56] I agree with him—because this is the context in which we see ourselves as we really are. We're exposed; we can't fake it just by going through the motions. God has been dealing with me in a deep way through the forty-four years I've been married, primarily through my wife and our relationship, and of course with our children and all that follows with it.

Years ago I was preparing to lead a marriage retreat. My wife and I had been married for about eight years, and we had two girls and a boy. I was in my study when the Holy Spirit asked me a question. It wasn't exactly audible, but I heard it: "Are you the kind of husband you want your daughters to marry?" I didn't like the kinds of answers that question provoked, but it was very helpful in clarifying my priorities.

TAKE A STAND FOR MARRIAGE AS A SOCIAL FOUNDATION

Did you know that the outcome of the push to make same-sex "marriage" legal might yet lie within your hands?

The struggle to desecrate the traditional understanding of marriage in our society reached a boiling-over point in February 2004, when the city of San Francisco filed a lawsuit against the state and flouted California law by issuing some four thousand marriage licenses to same-sex couples. In August 2004 the state high court upheld state law and annulled the city-issued licenses, but it was too late to lower the lid on Pandora's legal box. Massachusetts had already amended its state law in May 2004 to legalize same-sex marriages, and more states jumped into the fray.

In response to the California crisis, the Bush administration announced in February 2004 its endorsement of an amendment to the U.S. Constitution banning same-sex marriage. In the ensuing months, the American public was strangely quiet on the issue. Later that year I spoke personally with several members of Congress who were awaiting an outcry from their constituents, but it never came. Although most pro-family groups have endorsed the Marriage Protection Amendment, defining marriage exclusively as the union of one man and one woman, congressional support for the measure, while strong, has not yet reached the required two-thirds majority in either chamber.

Unless we are ready to see a judicially decreed, same-sex "marriage" hegemony imposed on the entire country, we must translate our outrage, conviction, and concern into phone calls to our elected officials. Unless Washington feels the heat from a groundswell of protest, they won't see the light, and marriage as we have known it in America will be further imperiled. I used to think the church was sleeping and that someday something big would happen, and we would all wake up and say, "Stop it now!" I still hope it will happen, but the hour is very late and the crisis is great.

Do you want to be a change agent? *Take a stand for the sanctity of marriage in our society.*

TAKE A STAND BY PARENTING YOUR KIDS PROACTIVELY

Newsweek magazine recently ran a cover story on the current generation's family crisis: parents who are finding it increasingly difficult to set limits for their children in a culture obsessed with buying and consuming things—and saturated with target marketing at children from corporations intent on building brand loyalty from "cradle to grave."[57]

Do you want to be a change agent? *Take a stand by parenting your kids proactively.*

There are many different dimensions to parenting, and my purpose here is not to list them all. Instead, through the lens of this article I want to take just one aspect that the culture itself recognizes as a major threat to the health of families and our children's future: setting limits. If you are married with children—or a close family friend or relative involved in the lives of children you love— take a look at your attitudes and behaviors in this area and consider where and how you can become an agent for positive change.

Teaching kids self-sufficiency. What are you doing to help today's children learn how to be self-sufficient in today's world instead of dependent on others to do things for them? "Kids who've been given too much too soon grow up to be adults who have difficulty coping with life's disappointments. They have a distorted sense of entitlement that gets in the way of success both in the workplace and in relationships. Psychologists say parents who overindulge their kids may actually be setting them up to be more vulnerable to future anxiety and depression."[58]

How are you modeling and teaching self-control? What are your opportunities for helping your kids learn how to overcome challenges by doing their own problem-solving and learning how and where to get help when they need it?

Spending quality AND quantity time with your children. "Baby boomers, raised in the contentious 1960s and 1970s (the era of the 'generation gap'), swore they would do things differently and have a much closer relationship with their own children. Many even wear the same Gap clothes as their kids and listen to the same music. 'So whenever their children get angry at them, it makes this generation feel a lot guiltier than previous generations,' says Laurence Steinberg, a psychologist at Temple University and the author of 'The 10 Basic Principles of Good Parenting.' Today's parents put in more hours on the job, too; at the end of a long workweek, it's tempting to buy peace with 'yes,' rather than mar precious family time with conflict."[59]

Do you allow guilt to drive any of your buying decisions for your kids? Do you default to anger instead of calm firmness in expressing *no*—and sticking to it? How do you protect family time during a long and busy week, when fatigue tempts you to tune out instead of tuning in—to your children, not to the television? "Most children need time, not money," comments Mary Pipher, author of *Raising Ophelia.* "What I mean is slow time, lying around on the floor being tickled, or reading a book, or making a salad."[60]

Assigning chores and imbuing a work ethic. "In their zeal to make their kids happy," the authors observe, "parents fail to impart the very values they say they want to teach. . . . What parents need to find, psychologists say, is a balance between the advantages of an affluent society and the critical life lessons that come from waiting, saving and working hard to achieve goals. That search for balance has to start early."[61]

The authors highlight a couple who tries to "walk the fine line between giving their children what they want and providing them with a strong enough work ethic so that they will become self-reliant."[62] The kids are expected to keep their grades up and set a goal for acceptance to a prestigious college or university. They must do chores as part of their family responsibilities—laundry, taking out the garbage, dishes, getting the mail, making coffee in the morning.

But families like this one are few and far between, say the authors. Far more common are parents who ask little or nothing of their kids, either because they think their kids are already over-whelmed with demands from school and activities or because it takes too much energy to enforce those responsibilities. "But kids who have no responsibilities never learn one of life's most basic lessons: that every individual can be of service to others and that life has meaning beyond one's own immediate happiness."[63]

What kinds of responsibilities have you assigned to your kids? What gives them tangible evidence that they are needed members of the family, capable of contributing to the family's well-being? How are you teaching them about the importance of putting others' needs above their own wants?

Modeling healthy choices about buying and consuming things. "By every measure, parents are shelling out record amounts. According to market researchers Packaged Facts, families with 3- to 12-year-olds spend $53.8 billion annually on entertainment, personal-care items and reading materials for their children. This is 17.6 billion more than parents spent in 1997. Teens are spending huge amounts of money themselves, some of it cadged from their families and the rest from after-school jobs. Last year 12- to 19-year-olds spent roughly $175 billion, $53 billion more than in 1997, according to Teen Research Unlimited. In the heat of this buying blitz, even parents who desperately need to say no find themselves reaching for their credit cards."[64]

Review what you have given to children for birthdays, Christmas, and special occasions in the last two years—and what else you have bought for them in between. Ask yourself, "What values have I communicated by choosing these gifts?"

How do you teach young children to manage money wisely—in giving, in saving, and in spending? How do you support older and adult children in learning to live within their means? How do they see these values modeled in the way you handle money?

Setting clear, firm boundaries. "In theory, setting limits with your children should be easy. In practice, though, when they beg and whine, it can be very tough. Minnesota parenting expert Jean Illsley Clarke came up with this handy crib sheet. Read it aloud. Then repeat.

1. No.
2. No, for sure.
3. No, and that's final.
4. No! Do not ask me again.
5. I have thought about it and the answer is no.
6. We don't have money for that right now."[65]

Make a list of your own script lines for setting boundaries and saying no. Which ones work well, and which ones don't? Read the following passage from the letter to the Hebrews, and ask yourself in what ways your discipline methods reflect God's view of discipline:

Endure hardship as discipline; God is treating you as sons. For what son is not disciplined by his father? If you are not disciplined (and everyone undergoes discipline), then you are illegitimate children and not true sons. Moreover, we have all had human fathers who disciplined us and we respected them for it. How much more should we submit to the Father of our spirits and live! Our fathers disciplined us for a little while as they thought best; but God disciplines us for our good, that we may share in his holiness. No discipline seems pleasant at the time, but painful. Later on, however, it produces a harvest of righteousness and peace for those who have been trained by it. (Hebrews 12:7–11)

"Permissive parenting is not just a thing of the past," cautions Ed Young:

It is still alive and well today—perhaps even in your own household. And while it may not sound so bad on the surface, there is a major problem with it. The problem is that permissive parenting doesn't work. Children are not designed to lead the family. They are not hardwired to call the shots or to handle that level of responsibility, because they do not have the maturity or the skill set to do so. Yet parent after parent resigns his or her leadership position, hands in the keys to the family study, and turns over the decision-making power to the child: "Where do *you* want to eat?" "What do *you* want to do tonight?"

"When do *you* want to go to bed?" "Where do *you* want to go on vacation?" "How may I serve *you?*" In short, they create a kid-CEO home. The kid-CEO household, however, is the opposite of God's dynamic design for the family.[66]

Take a look at your decisions over the past several months. Who is in charge in your family? In what ways, if any, does it resemble a Kid CEO household? In what ways does it resemble a Parent CEO household? Commit yourself to taking positive, proactive steps to parenting your kids responsibly. In perhaps no other area can you make a more critical contribution as a change agent.

TAKE A STAND BY GETTING INVOLVED

What characterizes those who get involved in our culture for Jesus Christ? They are . . .

- *Visionary*—they are able to see the needs of others.
- *Committed*—they get personally involved.
- *Tenacious*—they keep going no matter how long it takes to accomplish their purpose.
- *Focused*—they do not allow themselves to be distracted from their God-given purpose.
- *Overcomers*—they do not allow obstacles to stand in the way. They find a way to overcome those obstacles.
- *Compassionate*—they feel deeply the needs of others.
- *Courageous*—they do not become easily discouraged and, therefore, give up.

- *Risk takers*—they are willing to face embarrassment or misunderstanding by others to accomplish God's purpose.
- *Sacrificial*—they give of their time, their resources, and themselves.
- *Team players*—they may often work alone, but they know the importance of mutual encouragement and accountability with other believers.

The tipping point in a social epidemic such as revival does not occur because of sheer numbers of people getting involved. It begins with "the law of the few": an influential group of change agents who are willing to plant the seeds of the gospel. Through the work of the Holy Spirit an infectious agent in an environment can spread the "infection" rapidly.

Do you want to be a change agent? *Take a stand by getting personally involved.*

Think about the potential for change in this country if you and others you know began to take hold of a vision for a God-blessed America. What if just half of those Americans who claim to be evangelical Christians were truly to practice their faith—at home, at church, in their local communities, in responsible citizenship? With this kind of salt and light, every single volunteer social organization in this country seeking to meet the needs of less fortunate people would be transformed overnight. There would be so many volunteers they would have to be put on waiting lists.

The databases of crisis pregnancy centers and prison transition ministries and foster-care agencies would be crammed with the names and numbers of families ready to take in young women and ex-cons and children who need hospitality and practical help and loving care. Food pantry shelves would overflow. Homebound senior citizens would never be isolated. School children would have mentors for literacy programs and reading enrichment and adults committed to staying involved in their lives. Nursing-home residents would not pass time in empty days, neglected by family and ignored by society. Levels of financial giving to churches and ministries and charitable organizations would escalate.

When God pours out His blessings at a divine tipping point of His choosing, they will rain down on the saved and unsaved alike. Even those who are not influenced to accept Christ by such radical, positive changes in society would live better lives simply because of the culture's effects. What *would* those blessings look like?

The prophet Ezekiel, bringing God's Word to the Israelites exiled in Babylon, drew a beautiful picture of restoration that would occur when the corrupt shepherds of Israel were scattered and replaced by a ruler from David's line. The people had so defiled themselves—morally, spiritually, nationally—that God allowed them to suffer the consequences of national ruin, including the dreaded destruction of the beautiful temple in Jerusalem built during Solomon's reign. In the following passage, Ezekiel described how the people's lives would change when God restored them to relationship with Him. If you want to offer yourself to God as a change agent, consider taking this passage and turning it into a prayer for America:

> I will place over [my flock] one shepherd, my
> servant David, and he will tend them; he will tend
> them and be their shepherd. I the LORD will be their
> God, and my servant David will be prince among
> them. I the LORD have spoken.

I will make a covenant of peace with them and
rid the land of wild beasts so that they may live in
the desert and sleep in the forests in safety. I will
bless them and the places surrounding my hill. I will
send down showers in season; there will be showers
of blessing. The trees of the field will yield their fruit
and the ground will yield its crops; the people will
be secure in their land. They will know that I am the
LORD, when I break the bars of their yoke and rescue
them from the hands of those who enslaved them.
They will no longer be plundered by the nations, nor
will wild animals devour them. They will live in
safety, and no one will make them afraid. I will provide for them a land renowned for its crops, and they
will no longer be victims of famine in the land or
bear the scorn of the nations. Then they will know
that I, the LORD their God, am with them and that
they, the house of Israel, are my people, declares the
Sovereign LORD. You my sheep, the sheep of my pas-
ture, are people, and I am your God, declares the
Sovereign LORD." (Ezekiel 34:23–31)

TAKE A STAND WITH A VISION FOR RENEWAL

Change agents place their faith in Jesus Christ and have a fervent desire for the whole of their lives to reflect the power and
presence of their Lord and Savior. They recognize the transforming power of the gospel, and they are committed to seeing that
life-changing power revolutionize their own and their family's

lives, spreading outward to those in society who are without hope. They seek to be biblical witnesses in all areas of their lives, joining with other believers in bringing their moral and religious convictions into the public arenas of work, neighborhood, community, and nation.

In the face of a culture that denies the reality and the authority of the one true God, change agents are men and women of courage, not cowardice. They have set Christ at the crossroads of their lives, committing themselves to be His obedient followers in every step they take and in every decision they make.

I hope that after reading the previous few chapters you are struck with awareness of (1) our critical need for revival, and (2) the explosive potential of positive change in our country. My vision is for *an American society that affirms and practices Judeo-Christian values rooted in biblical authority.*

Will you share that vision with me?

My mission is to *awaken, inform, energize, equip, and mobilize Christians to be the catalysts for the biblically based transformation of their families, churches, communities, and nations.*

Will you join me? You may say I'm a dreamer, but I'm not the only one. The Lord Himself goes before us and is with us.

· 8 ·

Imagine! A society influenced by . . .

CHURCHES THAT REFLECT CHRIST, NOT CULTURE

Churches that reflect Christ, not culture, are really no different than people who are radical change agents. These distinctions are two sides of the same coin. That is because it is not possible to become all that God wants you to be apart from active service with and in a local assembly of believers where you are ministering to them the gifts God has given you, and they are ministering to you and other members of the body of Christ the gifts God has given them.

God did not create us to be "lone rangers." The fact that "it is not good for man to be alone" (Genesis 2:18) is not only true in marriage. God created us as social beings. Just as marriage is a divinely designed institution to meet the needs of a man and a woman for intimacy and procreation, so the church is a divinely designed institution to meet our needs for fellowship, personal growth, and adding new members to the family of Christ.

How Can the Church Have a Greater Influence on Culture?

Christians and churches that are obeying God's command to be salt and light will impact culture. Churches will reflect Christ when they are filled with Christians who reflect Christ. There is no way for the church to reflect Christ in its particular culture unless the Christians are reflecting Christ in that particular culture. Christians in churches who reflect Christ, not culture, can *change* culture. It isn't necessary that there be a hostile antithesis between church and culture in order for this to happen. In an America God is blessing, there would *not* be an antithesis.

Christians in the public square are bringing their faith into practice in the social sphere. My contention is that the culture should at least *accommodate* what Christians have to say. That standard is not high enough, maintains my colleague Jay Sekulow—the culture needs to *anticipate* what we have to say.

We will know that we are reaching a divine tipping point of blessing when the unsaved eagerly anticipate what we bring to the public square. Non-believers do not understand the things of God. They are foolishness to them because they can only be discerned spiritually (see 1 Corinthians 2). But when Christians speak publicly about the eternal truths of the Christian faith and God is healing the land, even the unsaved will respond, "You know, that's right."

It will not be the compelling nature of our arguments that wins the day; it will not even be the compelling example that we set. It will be the divine intervention on the minds and hearts of the whole culture, lost and saved. It will be *divine* persuasion. As Paul writes, "My message and my preaching were not with wise and persuasive words, but with a demonstration of the Spirit's power, so that your faith might not rest on men's wisdom, but on God's power" (1 Corinthians 2:4–5).

Our goal, therefore, is obedience: following in the footsteps of Jesus. When we are dedicated to being salt and light, we are always seeking to live the Christ-focused way. *God* will persuade the unsaved that this is the way to live. And they will eagerly anticipate what we have to say about problems facing this country. It will be a blessing of supernatural persuasion.

What we need to understand, therefore, is what radical obedience looks like: in our personal lives, in our family lives, in our local body of believers. Each local church is rightfully a body of Christ with Christ as its Head and Lord. It is composed of individuals who have experienced the radical, transforming love of Christ through being born again from above and who, together, are seeking to be more obedient disciples, who live lives that are more pleasing to their Savior, who give evidence in every area of their lives of being in love with Jesus.

In Revelation chapter 2, the church in Ephesus is praised for its hard work and perseverance while being charged with the sin of forsaking its first love. What does this mean for the church today? It is not enough to work diligently. It is not enough to be doctrinally sound. It is not enough to be moral. God is not satisfied unless we put our love for Jesus and our relationship with Him first in our lives. Such a church will be obedient to His teachings, but they will love sinners while hating the sin. They will condemn sin, not people. They will be eager to share the Savior who has transformed their lives with others. They will be characterized by evangelism, hospitality, generosity, a focus on ministry, a joyous way of living. Although they change the culture, they are part of a never-changing church, which worships a never-changing Savior, in an ever-changing world.

The separation of church and state was not Thomas Jefferson's idea, as is commonly thought. It comes to us from Roger Williams, who depicted the church as a garden amid the wilderness of the world. There had to be a wall protecting the garden of the church from the wilderness of the world, lest the wilderness encroach upon and choke out the garden. The church is an intentional counter-culture in which Christians are free to grow and develop and blossom, to disciple and be discipled.

The biblical analogy for the church that I like best is a colony of heaven: "But our citizenship is in heaven. And we eagerly await a Savior from there, the Lord Jesus Christ, who, by the power that enables him to bring everything under his control, will transform our lowly bodies so that they will be like his glorious body" (Philippians 3:20–21). Williams didn't think that the wall between the garden of the church and the wilderness of the world should be impenetrable, because although the purity of the garden was necessary for its own growth, the garden should seek to go out and domesticate the wilderness, so that more and more of the wilderness could become part of the garden. But there must always be a separation between the two.

We can't seek to make a church of America, because a church is made up of converted people, and the culture is never going to be entirely converted. But in a culture in which a significant percentage of Christians are practicing radical obedience both individually and collectively, it is going to be more difficult to do the wrong thing and easier to do the right thing. The right thing will be encouraged; the wrong thing will be discouraged.

RENEWAL AND REFORMATION IN THE BODY OF CHRIST

What will renewal and reformation in the body of Christ look like? It will start with the saved, because there aren't enough of us who are saved. There aren't enough of us who are saved and are acting like Christians. There aren't enough of us who are living lives in which our first priority is to do what is pleasing to Jesus.

We live in a world caught in a constant struggle between good and evil. We don't live in a neutral world. We live in a world in which the Devil prowls about like a roaring lion, seeking whom he may devour (1 Peter 5:8). He is able to disguise himself as an agent of light (2 Corinthians 11:14).

My wife couldn't tell you the number of times she has sat in her counseling office listening to confessions of unfaithfulness. Often they will say something like, "I can't believe I did that. What was I thinking? I just wanted to be happy!" They will often make these confessions while crying their eyes out—obviously, it didn't make them happy. They had bought the lie that what they craved would bring them what they truly wanted, which Satan had disguised to make it look so desirable that it appeared to justify their disobedience. Radical obedience means that you will follow the teachings of Jesus and the leading of the Holy Spirit in every area of your life. You will be seeking the Lord first; others, second; and yourself, third.

Every vocation is a calling from the Lord. Everyone is called. Therefore the question should be not "what do I want to do?" but "Lord, what have you created me to do?" There really should be no clerical collars. Those who are gifted for full-time ministry should be set aside to serve in ministry, so they don't have to be distracted by earning a living. As Martin Luther said, if you are a carpenter doing your work as a calling from the Lord, you can present a table you have made as an act of worship. We need to restore that understanding of calling and vocation.

Renewal in the body of Christ will bring a virtual end to the schismatic conflicts currently threatening the mainline denominations. Opposing camps will no longer be fighting one another, because those with unbiblical positions will either get saved or leave or be required to leave. Denominations practicing radical obedience will no longer be squabbling within, because those who are causing dissension will be dealt with biblically. Neither will there be dissension between denominations—healthy discussion, but not hostile disagreement.

I think it's helpful to distinguish areas of disagreement as primary, secondary, and tertiary. Primary areas include: was the Lord physically risen from the dead? A seminary student asked his professor, "How do I relate to a Christian who doesn't believe in the resurrection?" The professor replied, "You relate to him as a lost person." In areas of primary disagreement, there can be no compromise.

Areas of secondary disagreement are why we have denominations. For example, Baptists and Presbyterians disagree over whether baptism is a sacrament reserved for adults or practiced with infants. Others will organize themselves around styles of worship—informal or liturgical, or expressions of worship, such as glossolalia. It's better if they try not to worship in the same congregations, because it's going to make nobody happy.

Then there are areas of tertiary disagreement, such as the Calvinistic versus Armenian understanding of salvation. There is no reason why that should split a congregation. If you are practicing radical obedience, you will understand such secondary and tertiary differences, but you will not be spending your time trying to convince other groups of believers that they are wrong; you will be practicing truth, and you will be spending your time trying to convince the lost to get saved.

For radically obedient Christians, there should be no reason why these differences can't be set aside in order to make common cause in their stance vis-à-vis the culture. They will be agreed on abortion. They will be agreed on adultery. They will be agreed on homosexuality. They will be agreed on the need to be salt and light in the culture, practicing radical obedience. They will be agreed on what that obedience means for being a husband, a wife; a father, a mother; a son, a daughter; and a citizen.

Radically obedient Christians can make common cause on issues while they are worshipping in different congregations, but areas of disagreement will begin to dissolve as they come to a common understanding of the truth (until they all become

Baptists, in heaven). Racial segregation will be overcome because "there is neither Jew nor Greek, slave nor free, male nor female, for you are all one in Christ Jesus. If you belong to Christ, then you are Abraham's seed, and heirs according to the promise" (Galatians 3:28–29).

Socioeconomic segregation will cease because believers in our Lord Jesus Christ are not to show favoritism: "Suppose a man comes into your meeting wearing a gold ring and fine clothes, and a poor man in shabby clothes also comes in. If you show special attention to the man wearing fine clothes and say, 'Here's a good seat for you,' but say to the poor man, 'You stand there,' or 'Sit on the floor by my feet,' have you not discriminated among yourselves and become judges with evil thoughts?" (James 2:2–4).

In churches that are practicing radical obedience, divorce will be very rare. Premarital sex and adultery will be rare. These churches will have premarital counseling, preventing a lot of bad marriages from occurring. Their children will be taught from infancy on up that you don't marry non-Christians. That will prevent even more divorces. Everyone will be accepted as a person whom Jesus loves and for whom Jesus died, but that doesn't mean everyone's lifestyle will be accepted.

CHURCHES OF SALT AND LIGHT

First Baptist Church in Leesburg, Florida, has been practicing "needs-based" evangelism for nearly thirty years. Under the leadership of Senior Pastor Charles Roesel, the church has expanded to over seven thousand members and has consistently been in the top 1 percent of the nation in evangelism and mission giving. Pastor

Roesel travels frequently to other churches in order to teach the evangelistic method that has made First Baptist Leesburg a change agent in their community.

"Needs-based evangelism" reaches out to the unchurched by providing an array of services to meet practical needs of people in all sectors of society, opening up opportunities to address their greatest need for a relationship with Jesus Christ. First Baptist Leesburg has created a "ministry village" with seven different centers of specific ministry:

- A women's shelter providing transitional support for displaced women and their young children, often victims of abuse, neglect, or homelessness. The church provides personal counseling, financial planning, childcare and nutrition education, help in finding jobs and permanent housing, and life-skills instruction for life upon leaving the shelter. The women's center works with local community services to help the women and their children become independent. Along with the practical assistance, the ministry provides spiritual counsel and encouragement.

- A primary care medical center cosponsored by the church and the Central Florida Health Care Foundation. Thousands of patients have received medical services from professionals and volunteers, available to any resident of the community who has financial need and is without health insurance.

- A residential children's shelter for kids aged six through twelve who have been displaced by abuse and neglect. As children continue to suffer the consequences of escalating divorces, teenage pregnancies, substance abuse, domestic

abuse, poverty, and unemployment, the shelter provides
transitional care while the children's living arrangements
are determined.

- A residential teen shelter for young people aged thirteen
through seventeen.
- A pregnancy care center providing free pregnancy tests,
assistance with baby clothes and baby-care items, distribution of car seats, adoption counseling and adoption refer-
rals, childbirth/nutrition classes, post-abortion counseling,
parenting classes, and financial planning.
- A men's rescue mission with multiple beds, a twelve-week
substance abuse program, and an economic program. This
center helps men deal responsibly with their problems,
find work, establish independent living arrangements, and
get assimilated into church and community. It also serves
dinner to needy families on Thanksgiving Day.
- A benevolence center providing food, clothing, financial
assistance, and financial counseling for those who need
help with electric, gas, and rental bills.
- A Christian school for grades K–12, certified by the
Association of Christian Schools International, dedicated to
equipping students spiritually for service in the body of
Christ, morally for citizenship in the United States of
America, and academically for success in higher education
or their chosen vocation.
- A performing arts academy offering classes in music,
dance, art, and musical theater.

- A street ministry including visitation to schools, private homes, hospitals, jails, sponsorship of youth camps, and support to needy families during holiday seasons.
- A day care facility with a sliding scale of fees based on financial need.
- Anyone in the community can go to that church and find help, extended to them in the name and in the love of Christ. It is irresistible.

Sagemont Baptist Church in Houston, Texas, is another example of a church practicing radical obedience. One evening, an apartment near the church burned down. Before the fire trucks had left, the pastor and his ministry staff had arrived and were handing out $500 checks to every family affected. There were no strings attached—but they weren't necessary. This tangible demonstration of the love of Christ brought a lot of those families into the church and into relationship with Jesus Christ.

Sagemont maintains a "helping hands" ministry for all church members, modeling the way they believe the body of Christ should operate. A storehouse is maintained to provide free items: food, furniture, clothing, appliances, toys, household supplies, tools, automobiles. No one who comes for help is turned away, and those who receive from this ministry are then asked to join a Bible study to ensure they are immersed in the Word and growing in the Lord.

Free services available to members include CPA counsel for tax questions; lawyers for help with wills, trusts, estates, contracts, and purchase agreements; doctors of all specialties to render medical aid, recommendations, or information in times of uncertainty; computer experts who design and maintain the church's programs and hardware; plumbers, carpenters, painters, roofers, mechanics, electricians, and others who aid the widows and elderly; teachers for remedial tutoring to children who are falling behind in their studies; bankers who help people learn how to handle their money; insurance agents who regularly provide industry information to help make informed decisions.

Among the many ministries at Willow Creek Church in South Barrington, Illinois, is a Saturday auto shop for single and divorced women who can bring their cars for repairs and maintenance by men in the church.

CAFETERIA CHRISTIANS

Being salt and light in our culture means obedience in *all* areas of life. Some Christians try to pick and choose which parts of the faith they want to accept, or which applications of it seem acceptable or unacceptable to them. We live in a time of great moral crisis, requiring us to stand firm against the evils of our day. Compromise erodes our witness and weakens the influence of the church. For example, trying to accommodate the culture by supporting family values while compromising on the issue of abortion is not radical obedience—it's failure to repent and turn from our wicked ways.

There's far too much "cafeteria-style" Christianity in the body of Christ today. American consumers have grown so accustomed to the luxury of choices in every area of life that it has seeped into our churches. We want Jesus as a friend, as a personal Savior for a private faith, as a financial counselor, a marriage counselor—a *guidance* counselor. However, obedience means that we want Jesus as *Lord,* and that we invite His lordship into every nook and cranny of our lives, seen and unseen, private and public.

Have you been practicing cafeteria-style Christian faith in any areas of your life? Has guilt or fear kept you from humbling your-self before the Lord because there are some parts of your life you don't want to confront? Perhaps it's time for a spiritual spring cleaning.

There's an old poem I can still recall snatches of—"Oh, I wish there was someplace called the land of beginning again, where I could take all my broken dreams and heartaches and drop them at the door like a shaggy old coat, and never put it on again." Well, there is a place called the Land of Beginning Again—it's found at the foot of the cross.

We serve a Lord of New Beginnings. With whom did God choose to make an everlasting covenant? Abraham, a coward and a liar.[67]

Who was the one to whom God chose to give the Ten Commandments, including the command, "Thou shalt not kill"? Moses, a murderer.[68]

Who was the chosen leader with whom God covenanted that his offspring would one day yield the Messiah? David, an adulterer and an accessory to murder.[69]

And to whom was Jesus referring when he said "on this rock I will build my church"? (Matthew 16:18). Peter, a man who would curse him and deny him.

Your past does not determine your future. Spring cleaning means second chances. But the opportunity for second chances does not mean compromising doctrine. God forgave Moses, but He didn't let him see the Promised Land. God forgave David, but

He didn't let him build the temple. Your life isn't over when you commit a grave sin, but there are always consequences.

I have a good friend I would have named if you had asked me a few years ago, "Who are the top five Christian leaders you are absolutely sure would never fall into sexual sin?" He's now selling cars. Yes, he can be restored, but he will never be what he could have been.

Paul said, "I do not run like a man running aimlessly; I do not fight like a man beating the air. No, I beat my body and make it my slave so that after I have preached to others, I myself will not be disqualified for the prize" (1 Corinthians 9:26–27). There are things you can do that disqualify you for leadership in the ministry. Can you be forgiven? Yes. Can God give you a tremendous ministry? Yes. Can you be restored as if it had never happened? No.

We have to make a distinction between leadership in the church and other areas of ministry. Can you be restored to being a church member in full standing, leading a godly life, being tremendously blessed in serving God? Yes. Can you be restored to being in a position of pastoral authority? No.

These are realities in the church that must be dealt with in order for us to continue practicing radical obedience. Our focus, however, should not be on what we *can't* do, but on what God *can* do through us. Then repentance from sin and seeking the Lord's will in our lives will not be a teeth-gritting exercise of personal will power; it will be a relief to turn our back on our own ways and seek God's ways instead. Only when we have refused to surrender to the lordship of Christ does sin retain its power over us. Dallas Willard identifies what makes the difference in viewing radical obedience as an impossible standard versus a joyous way of life:

> To the person who is not inwardly transformed in each essential dimension, evil and sin still *look good*. They are strongly attractive. That is precisely what Peter calls, "the corruption that is in the world through strong desire or lust" (2 Peter 1:4 [paraphrased]). To such people the law is hateful because it denies them what they have their hearts set on; and everything must then be done to evade the law and do what they want. The force of their whole being is set against Christlikeness, even if they do suffer from a bad conscience that tells them they are in the wrong.
>
> As Jesus trains them and "cleanses them for himself," however, all of that begins to reverse. The law begins to appear as a beautiful gift of God, as precious truth about what is really good and right. It becomes, in the language of the psalmist, "sweeter than honey freshly dripping from the honeycomb" (Psalm 19:10 [paraphrased]; honey never again tastes as good as when freshly taken). At that point it is sin that looks stupid, ridiculous, as well as repulsive—which it really is. Resistance to sin is then based upon that new and realist vision of what it is, not on fear of punishment. The illusion that sin is really a good thing arbitrarily prohibited by God is

dispelled, and we see with gratitude that his prohibitions are among his greatest kindnesses.[70]

There are good reasons why God ordained the institution of the body of Christ. We need one another for accountability, encouragement, and partnership in our common role as radical change agents. Let Paul's closing charge in his epistle to the Ephesians be your rallying cry:

> God is strong, and he wants you strong. So take everything the Master has set out for you, well-made weapons of the best materials. And put them to use so you will be able to stand up to everything the Devil throws your way. This is no afternoon athletic contest that we'll walk away from and forget about in a couple of hours. This is for keeps, a life-or-death fight to the finish against the Devil and all his angels.
>
> Be prepared. You're up against far more than you can handle on your own. Take all the help you can get, every weapon God has issued, so that when it's all over but the shouting you'll still be on your feet. Truth, righteousness, peace, faith, and salvation are more than words. Learn how to apply them. You'll need them throughout your life. God's Word is an *indispensable* weapon. In the same way, prayer is essential in this ongoing warfare. Pray hard and long. Pray for your brothers and sisters. Keep your eyes open. Keep each other's spirits up so that no one falls behind or drops out. (Ephesians 6:10–18 *The Message*)

Imagine! An America that is . . .

LIBERATED FROM THE CULT OF SELF

You don't have to look far in pop culture to notice that it really is "all about *me*."

Our age-obsession has taken a new twist recently by extolling the sex appeal of older women as celebrity actresses appear to age gracefully in the public eye. Older actresses are receiving praise (and protest) for their willingness to expose themselves in revealing scenes on stage and film. It is considered fun and entertaining for women in their sixties and seventies to pose in discreetly blocked nudity for fund-raising calendars. The conventional pattern of older male celebrities marrying women young enough to be their daughters and granddaughters has been inverted as a form of protest: movies are currently proliferating in which older women wield powerful sex appeal over younger men.

A recent article in *More* magazine, targeted at the second-half-of-life female population, featured a profile of actress Annette Bening. Although she is known for a number of starring roles in feature films, her tabloid popularity has been based on her achievement in taming the infamously womanizing Warren Beatty with an apparently monogamous marriage to her. The article was timed to coincide with the release of Bening's latest film, *Being Julia*, featuring an aging actress who has an adulterous affair with a much younger male actor. When the actor ends the affair by dumping her for a younger woman, the aging diva takes an emotional dive.

The triumph of the film, according to this article, is that the aging actress "pulls herself together" to find a way to wreak public vengeance upon her former lover's new flame—on stage. Getting even instead of getting depressed is apparently the paradigm for maturity in this story: "There comes a point in your life where you can either choose to mature or not," observed Bening in discussing her character. "And maybe, in a way, that's what middle age is all about. . . . This is a woman of enormous talent and enormous creativity. Over the course of the movie, she grows up. And she finds simple pleasure in being alive and knowing herself better."[71] Of course there is no mention that the central character in this movie had committed adultery, nor of the double standard that she was happy for the casual sex when it gratified her but enraged when someone else dared to do the same thing at her expense.

Perhaps what is most revealing, however, is that Bening and the writer of the article laud one particular scene as "pivotal" in the character's liberation and growth. The diva has of course been on a perpetual diet, and one evening she dares to go to dinner all by herself and break her diet by drinking a beer. In this "bold" act, she discovers that she enjoys her own company. "In that moment," writes the article's author, "she transforms from a 20th-century to a 21st-century heroine." Bening comments, "Julia's ultimate triumph isn't really her moment of revenge. Her triumph is in being alone and learning how to be with herself and know herself."[72]

Is *this* the evidence of our cultural advance into a new century—hero-worship of an adulterous, vengeful woman whose pinnacle of growth is enjoying intimacy with herself while she throws off cultural pressure by drinking a beer in defiance of her dieting? Clearly we live in a society obsessed with—deliriously *inebriated* with—the idol of Self.

Our insatiable appetite for the praise of men, however, means that the idol of Self must itself bow to the latest trends. Blatant attempts to earn social approval and status would look embarrassingly passé these days. Therefore, it has become fashionable to denounce pretense and espouse some version of "be who you really are," as the *More* magazine article so clearly illustrates.

The catch is that wealthy celebrities tend to indulge publicly in such sentiments only after they have undergone cosmetic surgeries to enhance their features and change their body parts, taken extended spa vacations designed to pamper the body and recapture a sense of youthful vigor, and hired a bevy of personal-care managers to perfect their appearance. Better still if you can snag another celebrity whose wealth and social status increase your own exponentially. I intend no criticism of Ms. Bening here, simply an observation of the value system in which she so prominently figures.

Thanks to technological developments, our frantic pursuit of never-ending self-enhancement now extends to the possibility of cloning oneself—paying someone to store your DNA in order to grow new body parts or bring you back to life in some mythical future when human beings have succeeded in their ability to create and sustain the good life.

This is an old story. It's entitled, "False Visions of Purpose and Meaning and Happiness." It is the recurring story of the Tower of Babel—humanity's attempt to reach up and become God.

We have many subplots to this story today: the false vision of euphoria that has ensnared so much of our population in substance abuse . . . the antiaging, beauty-makeover, remake-yourself lure of boosting your market value for better relationships, better jobs, better lifestyles . . . the fantasy of easy sex as the fulfillment of your deepest longings . . . the temptation to secure an elite place in the social order by the jewelry you wear, the clothing brands you display, the house you live in, the kind of car you drive, the spouse you were able to snag.

All of it is focused on Self: self-fulfillment, self-medication, self-preoccupation, self-centered living. Where your heart is, there your treasure will be also. American culture has moved away from a sanctity-of-life foundation to a quality-of-life foundation. We no longer treasure people for their inherent value as human beings; we treasure them only if they meet certain superficial characteristics that feed our false visions of purpose and meaning and happiness.

For example, "lookism" is alive and well in the United States. This is prejudice against some people and in favor of others based solely on their physical appearance. We have lots of physical prejudices in this culture. We are prejudiced in favor of male verticality. Men who are vertically challenged are not as successful with women, and they don't get promoted as much. CEOs are significantly taller than the average population. The phrase "tall, dark and handsome" didn't just come out of the thin air. We ascribe values of physical power to men, and values of sexual appeal to women. Feminine attractiveness is defined by the impossibly proportioned Barbie doll. And so we have women endangering their health with cosmetic surgery to add here and tuck there . . . young girls throwing away their lives with eating disorders . . . older women desperate to look younger.

In an America God was blessing, "lookism" would be on its deathbed. We would be more concerned with character, inner beauty, how we treat others, the good works we can do with time and money—serving others instead of self-serving.

There's a difference between being influenced by your culture and being driven by your culture. It is inevitable that you will be influenced by your culture. But it is not inevitable that your choices in life will be driven by your culture. You are the only one who can determine which it will be.

UNDERSTAND YOUR CULTURAL INFLUENCES

All of us are influenced and shaped by our surrounding culture. Each generation lives in a different period of history, collects a different set of memories, undergoes changes at a different rate, and is shaped by a different prevailing worldview, or *Zeitgeist*. Collectively, the people in a given generation have a cultural identity that differs from the generation that came before them and from the generation that follows after them.

The World War II generation, for example, was shaped by a particular set of formative events—largely involving hardship, deprivation, struggle, and the upheaval of a prolonged war fought in multiple theaters against two aggressor nations. My parents have been deeply and permanently shaped by the Great Depression. As a consequence, no matter how good things are, they always remember how bad it can be—in a way that the Boomer generation cannot.

The Boomers can't really comprehend the reality of the Great Depression, because they didn't live through it. Their cultural materialism is based on an assumption that they are entitled to affluence, as if they were born on third base because they had hit a triple, when all they did was get born on third base.

The Millennial generation that has been fighting the war in Iraq in 2003–2004 cannot comprehend the Vietnam War. When Ted Kennedy spoke of this war with Iraq as "another Vietnam," his statement had virtually no impact on people other than those between ages 45 and 55—half of the Boomer generation. Those of us who lived through the Vietnam War as draft-age people have a collective generational experience we need to recognize as such. Sometimes that cognitive experience is a good thing; sometimes it's a bad thing; sometimes it's a neutral thing. But it is always there, and we need to be examining it so we can ask, "What part of my thinking in this case is Christian, and what part of it is cultural?"

For example, let's take a look at how differently generations think about war. My father was born in 1922. He joined the Navy at eighteen and fought in World War II. I am from the Vietnam War generation. Had I gone to him and told him that I was going to evade the draft by moving to Canada, as many young men did at the time, he would have disowned me. Many in my father's generation viewed military service as an unquestioned duty that men owed their country—Christians especially would never shirk such a responsibility.

I honor all our men and women who served in Vietnam. If I had been drafted, I would have served my country, even though I was a "hawk" on that war and felt that our government let down our military by not supporting them fully in the field.

However, if the government came after *my* son to draft him, and I didn't feel that the war was just or that the government was fully committed to it, I would help my son go to Canada as a protest if he shared those views and desired to do so. My attitude toward the government has been fundamentally and irretrievably altered by the Vietnam experience, just as my father's attitude toward the government was fundamentally and irretrievably forged by his experience of World War II.

I think these are morally neutral distinctions. They are just part and parcel of a generational experience.

Another way to understand cultural identity is to ask, "What is our cultural experience as Americans?" It's very different from the cultural experience of someone living in the Third World, or on the European continent.

When my wife and I visited Switzerland, we stayed in a picturesque little village tucked way up in the mountains. The innkeeper told us that there was going to be a native dance festival, with participants clad in their traditional clothing—lederhosen, peasant blouses, colorful skirts, and so on. Native pride, we were told, was rooted in the tradition of living all your life in the same village you were born in, and taking up the same trade your parents worked in. If your father was a watchmaker, then you became a watchmaker. If your family raised cows, then you raised cows. "That's awful!" I said to my wife. "How can they *stand* it?"

"Because you're the one who thinks it's awful," my wife answered. "You're an American. Americans believe that individuals should have the right to make their own choices about where they live and what they do. We're not bound by our birth or our social class. We are free to be who we want to be—it's our inalienable right to life, liberty, and the pursuit of happiness. But these people are happy with this—it's normal for them; it's comfortable. They would feel very threatened by the laissez-faire, survival-of-the-fittest approach to making their way in life."

Well, she's right! I thought. *But I AM an American, and this is awful!*

That's not a theological issue; that's a cultural issue.

But what about the American cultural value, which has been taught to us in so many different ways, that the key to happiness and self-fulfillment is the acquisition and consumption of material things and satisfying experiences?

That's *not* just a cultural issue. It's a theological issue, because it's focused on self.

The American right to life, liberty, and the pursuit of happiness can be interpreted in different ways. A Christian take on it would be that yes, we are certainly free to pursue these things, and government doesn't have the right to interfere with our pursuit. But God certainly has the right to interfere with it, to tell us what the limits of our liberty are, how that liberty is to be pursued, and how to define happiness. Our society has run seriously amok in its relationship to wealth, status, and sex. The cultural myths that we live with—that what's important is youth, appearance, body type, the kind of car we drive, how big a house we can afford, what kind of job we have—are all related to one of those three categories: wealth, status, or sex.

In this culture, the acquiring of wealth is the way we keep score and status—"how much is he worth?" The Christian community is not immune to this, either. Years ago there was a movie starring Dick van Dyke called "Cold Turkey," in which he played a Methodist minister who got the whole town to quit smoking suddenly, himself included. It became a national phenomenon, and he got on the cover of *Time* magazine. His bishop called him in and said to him, "My son, it's difficult to measure success in our business." Then he held up a copy of *Time* magazine and said, "But *this* is success!"

French philosopher Alain de Botton has made a career out of asking people hard questions and writing books about his findings. Book reviewer Jason Byassee points out that "his newest book, *Status Anxiety,* offers a historical response to why people in modern Western democracies feel so anxious when they have so much luxury compared to what even the wealthiest enjoyed in earlier ages. His diagnosis: Since we live in a supposed meritocracy, there seems no one but ourselves to blame if we do not amass as much stuff or as many accolades as our neighbors. We are just 'losers,' to use our culture's most 'chillingly contemptuous word.' We chase status as though it were a form of love, which it indeed seems to be."[73]

How many times have you heard somebody called to a church that was smaller and paid less? Do we think that the Holy Spirit never does that? I suspect that the Holy Spirit does it more often than we know.

What's different about cultural values for a Christian living in an upper-class neighborhood versus a Christian living in an inner-city neighborhood? While I was attending an inner-city church in Texas, I heard about a pastor in another inner-city church that was in a very difficult neighborhood. I wanted to ask him to speak at one of our seminars, so I went to hear him preach.

I took my wife and son and oldest daughter with me. When this pastor began his sermon, he spoke passionately about drugs. It was clear that drugs, gang wars, and life-and-death struggles were a part of his and his congregation's everyday existence in a way that was not part of our family's or our congregation's.

Then he launched into a direction that made us feel like intruders on a family discussion. "Now I know that some of you women have gone back to school and gotten your degrees and you've moved up in the world," he said. "And you're embarrassed by your husbands. You're embarrassed that he's an auto mechanic, and he doesn't speak correct English, and you think you have the right to get yourself a trophy husband."

In his subculture, black women were far more likely than black men to be upwardly mobile, and to use education as a means of improving their socioeconomic status. He had an issue with Christian women being embarrassed by their husbands' lack of status and social behavior in the same way that my subculture had an issue with older, successful men being tempted to trade in their wives for younger trophy models who would be better at meeting their libido needs. Both these patterns are rooted in the assumption that status and wealth and power will bring happiness. This is just self-fulfillment—"I have to find myself." Jesus said, "Lose yourself. That's the way to find happiness" (see Matthew 16:25). Radical obedience is about doing His will, not yours.

"But I Just Want to Be Happy"

I don't think we have to encourage a healthy sense of self—it comes with the sin nature. No one has to be taught to be focused on self. If you are concerned with radical obedience, that will take care of itself. Who knows what's best for us? Do we know what's best, or does the Lord? It's a silly question, but we keep asking it in the way we live.

A young woman came to see me about getting married. I knew both her and her fiancée, and they had "disaster" stamped on their foreheads. During our first pre-marital counseling session, they got into a big fight over checkbooks.

I begged her not to get married.

She did, and a year later she came back to me and said, "You were right. I didn't marry the right person. But I have found the right person now, and we believe it's God's will for me to leave my husband, for him to leave his wife, and for us to get married. What do you think?"

I told her what I thought.

"But I just want to be happy!" she said.

"Who knows best what's going to make you happy?" I asked her. "You, or God? God created you. He knows more about who you are than you do. He created you to fulfill a unique purpose that He has for your life. Who knows better how that purpose is going to be fulfilled—you or God?"

We are by nature pleasure-seeking creatures. There's a difference between pleasure and happiness. It's alright to have happiness as a goal—the point is how you define happiness. God says happiness is being in the center of His will and knowing Him and pleasing Him.

Dr. Ed Young talks about how people tend to go into marriage. She says, "I want him to meet all my needs," and he says, "I want her to meet all my needs." He calls that the tick-and-dog syndrome. A tick gets on a dog and saps all the energy out of it. So you have two ticks at the altar and no dog, because each one is going to end up sapping the energy out of the other. They forget that the primary purpose of marriage is not to get your own needs met, but to meet the needs of your mate.

But what do you do if you're in a marriage with a spouse who is not able or willing to invest in the marriage according to what God wants for marriage? Decades go by, and you realize that apart from a miracle of the Holy Spirit, it ain't gonna get any better. Is happiness possible?

It can be. Corrie ten Boom was in a concentration camp, and she was happy. Peter counsels us, "Cast all your anxieties on him because he cares for you" (1 Peter 5:7). He might change your circumstances, or He might change you.

Ask yourself: "Who determines my happiness—my spouse, or God?"

You can be happy just knowing that you are being obedient to the Lord, and you are pleasing Him. I've known lots of people in long-term, difficult marriages, and some of them are the most radiantly, incandescently happy people I have ever met.

Your only alternative is the declaration, "In order for me to be happy, this person must meet my expectations and needs." That assumption makes this other person determinative of God's ultimate will over your life—that's theologically indefensible.

Your happiness is not dependent on circumstances. It is dependent on your reaction to those circumstances. Marriage is the place where our culturally mistaken ideas about happiness and sex get intertwined most thoroughly. Most people get married thinking, *This person will make me happier.* The Christian should get married thinking, *I believe it is God's will for me to marry this person, and I'm going to do my best to make this person happy.* But the honest truth is that most people, Christians included, get married thinking, *I have found the person who will make me happy.*

Sometimes we need to ask ourselves, "How did I get into this situation in the first place?" One young woman admitted to me, "I wouldn't be in this difficult marriage if my relationship with the Lord had been strong at the time." That doesn't excuse a spouse's abusive behavior, but it does point to the consequences we bring on by our own choices.

Ask yourself, "Does my happiness depend on my circumstances, or does it depend on my relationship with the Lord?" When you put it like that, it's a pretty basic question—simple, even. But simple is not easy. Great fallacies have been built on the assumption that *simple* and *easy* are synonyms. They're not. There are a lot of things that are simple but are not easy. And there are a lot of things that are easy but not simple.

We grow up thinking that our happiness is dependent on our accumulation and experience of wealth, status, and attractiveness to the opposite sex. It's the American dream, and it runs through all levels and spheres of society—the sports industry, the pecking order in a high school, the workplace, the media. We're sold that dream, and then we are continually being sold products that supposedly will make that dream come true.

I remember hearing Johnny Carson remark, on the eve of his fourth marriage, that people think money buys happiness, but it doesn't, he said. It just eliminates some of the things you have to worry about. Once you acquire wealth and power, how do you ever know whether you are loved for yourself, or for your ability to transfer that wealth and power to others?

We are told incessantly that the path to happiness is to have as much satisfying sex as possible and to consume as many material goods as we can obtain. If we could just have enough money to fulfill all our material wants in an ever-expanding universe, and if we could just have—for men, as wild and diverse and satisfying sex as possible, and for women, a loving, caring, exclusive, committed, and mutually nurturing relationship, then we would be happy.

Deprogramming from the Cult of Self

The largest cult in America is the cult of Self. It's hard to get out of this cult, because this cult comprises the entire culture, not just one small group of individuals. Most Americans are starving for spiritual nourishment, because they keep trying to satisfy their spiritual hunger with material things and they keep trying to find their purpose and meaning for existence in an intimate relationship. These cravings for sexual satisfaction and material goods are versions of idolatry—the attempt to get our deepest needs met by something other than God, the desire to turn to something or someone other than God to find happiness. God doesn't bless idolatry; he curses it.

To deprogram from this cult of Self, you can start by taking inventory with the Big C's—your checkbook and your calendar.

If you want to know how much you are influenced by our society's false visions of purpose, meaning, and happiness, sit down with your checkbook register for the last three months and ask yourself, "What are my values?"

If you are evaluating your priorities, you might affirm, "God comes first; my spouse and family are second; my career is third." Then sit down with your calendar for the last three months and add up the amount of time you spent on daily devotions, in worship, in Bible study, with your family, on your career, on yourself. Then ask yourself, "What are my priorities?"

Most Americans live in houses bigger than they need. Few families need to live in a five-thousand-square-foot house, unless they have as many as ten children. Far too often we look on our houses as more than just a place to live. That's why in real estate, the three most valuable criteria are location, location, and location. We want to move up to the neighborhood that reflects the comfort level we feel we have earned, the measure of success we have achieved. We want to live with people who have similar taste and discrimination. Would Jesus live in a gated community in order to separate Himself from those who weren't at the same income and education level? Of course not!

Do we look on cars as status symbols, or as a means of transportation? Do we have car payments because we couldn't come up with the cash to get what we needed, or do we have car payments because we wanted more car than we could afford or need? Most Americans own more cars than they need to drive, and drive bigger cars than they need to own.

Most of us have far more clothes than we need—more furniture, more dishes, more food in the refrigerator. We buy bigger television screens and more cable channels. We spend money eating out because it's convenient or entertaining. We spend money storing stuff we can't fit in our homes.

A life of radical obedience would be a lot simpler—less ostentatious, less energy-consuming. I'm not suggesting that we all go on witch hunts to find out who is living the most radically obedient lifestyle. On its own, the size of your television screen may have absolutely nothing to do with whether you are living in radical obedience to the Lord. The question here is balance, and I think most of us would agree that Americans—American Christians included—tend to lean more heavily on the side of material comfort, personal ease, and social status in our consumption.

If pets bring pleasure and joy into your life, I'm not saying it's wrong to spend money on them—it depends on whether you have other priorities in balance in your life. But if you have a dog, does it have to be a certain kind of dog? Does it have to have a pedigree so advanced that if the dog could read it, it wouldn't talk to you? And if so, *why* do you feel the need to spend thousands of dollars on a dog with papers?

It is not a sin to drive a BMW or a Mercedes. But if you get your self-worth from what others think of you, instead of from what

Jesus thinks of you, and that is why you bought a prestigious car or a trendy canine breed, then perhaps you are being held captive to the American cult of Self.

YOUR LIBERATION IS AT HAND

The only healthy sense of self is a biblical understanding of identity. You are the special creation of God, made in His own image. But you cannot on your own live as God intended you to live, because the original cult of Self cast its first shadow on the very dawn of human history. Sin entered the world when Adam and Eve used their freedom to choose Self over God, separating the human race from perfect union with its Creator. You inherited this fallen nature when you were born into the human race, and the moment you became capable of moral action, you became a transgressor of God's law, under condemnation. You were also born into an environment already inclined toward sin, a world that has rejected the grace of God and is busy trying to recruit you for the ranks of those who have chosen rebellion over surrender.

In Jesus Christ, God broke the chains binding you to the wretched cult of Self, so that you might choose freely to be restored to relationship with Him and inherit eternal life instead of eternal separation from God. That new life begins the moment you receive the free gift of salvation by accepting Jesus Christ as your personal Lord and Savior. You become a new creature in Christ, a member of God's family. The saving grace of God in Jesus Christ will now empower you to live a life worthy of your calling as a child of God. Paul explains exactly how this empowerment happens in Romans 8:5–14:

Those who live according to the sinful nature
have their minds set on what that nature desires; but
those who live in accordance with the Spirit have
their minds set on what the Spirit desires. The mind
of sinful man is death, but the mind controlled by
the Spirit is life and peace; the sinful mind is hostile
to God. It does not submit to God's law, nor can it do
so. Those controlled by the sinful nature cannot
please God.

You, however, are controlled not by the sinful
nature but by the Spirit, if the Spirit of God lives in
you. And if anyone does not have the Spirit of
Christ, he does not belong to Christ. But if Christ is
in you, your body is dead because of sin, yet your
spirit is alive because of righteousness. And if the
Spirit of him who raised Jesus from the dead is living
in you, he who raised Christ from the dead will also
give life to your mortal bodies through his Spirit,
who lives in you.

Therefore, brothers, we have an obligation—but
it is not to the sinful nature, to live according to it.
For if you live according to the sinful nature, you
will die; but if by the Spirit you put to death the mis-
deeds of the body, you will live, because those who
are led by the Spirit of God are sons of God.

Your inward transformation through the indwelling Spirit of
God is the foundation of lasting change not only in your life, but
in human society—because all Christians are under obligation to

seek to make the will of Christ supreme not only in their own lives, but in human society. And the only way to bring true change to our desperate, self-centered, and self-imprisoned world is by the grace of God in Jesus Christ. You can spend all day long dreaming up means and methods for improving society and promoting moral values. But unless those means and methods are rooted in the regeneration of individuals who have embraced the gospel and are living out their faith, social action alone will never accomplish permanent change.

Renounce membership in the cult of Self. Take inventory to see where its influences may have crept into your life, and offer those areas to God in repentance, asking Him to transform you into a servant of Christ in all areas of your life. Imagine God's blessing upon you . . . and fellow believers . . . and new Christians who hear and accept the Good News through the ministry of servants who labor in the harvest . . . as together your influence spreads throughout a sin-sickened culture, cleansing it and transforming it so that millions of people can rise from the death of Self to life in the Spirit. Let us set our sights on nothing less than a glorious reformation of our culture, preparing for the return of Christ not by turning our backs on the world, but by turning our faces to God that we might bring healing to our land.

· 10 ·

Imagine! A nation shaped by . . .

COMMITMENT TO THE
COMMON GOOD

What would our country look like if the divine tipping point were reached and showers of blessing rained down on the righteous and unrighteous alike? We have already explored the possibilities for changes in our culture at the most fundamental levels of belief, thought, and behavior: if every believer grasped how important his or her individual faith is in shaping our culture and determining the future of our country; if our nation consistently valued the sanctity of every human life; if we understood human sexuality and honored it instead of perverting it; if stable and happy marriages were the norm; if children were cherished, raised in loving homes with both parents, and nurtured instead of victimized by adults; if Christians who understood the importance of their faith committed themselves to becoming change agents in every sphere of life; if churches became change agents in community, reflecting life in Christ, not life as our secular culture lives it; if our country were free of its obsession with self.

Imagine all that—and then think of what the implications are for the kind of government we would have; for the values driving our economy; for the way we treat the environment. In government, the common good would be valued above individual power, status, and politics. In the economy, money and power would not be the supreme values. In our treatment of the environment, we would operate as stewards instead of owners. The impulses to dominate, control, exploit, and consume would be replaced by impulses to serve, look on others' interests as more important than our own, to be good stewards of what is entrusted to our care, to practice gratitude for the gifts we have and giving to those in need.

A Trustworthy Government

"Congress shall make no law respecting an establishment of religion, or prohibiting the free exercise thereof." Thus begins the First Amendment to the Constitution of the United States of America. At first reading these words seem to be a remarkable example of both clarity and brevity. Yet Americans have spent an enormous amount of time and effort over the past two centuries trying to decipher the "original intent" of the original ratifiers of the amendment. Sixteen words consisting of two clauses, known respectively as the "establishment" and the "free exercise" clauses, dealing with one subject, government, and one object, religious liberty. Why can't Americans decide what these sixteen words mean? Why has the struggle to define and apply the First Amendment's "freedom of religion" escalated into one of the most heated and volatile battlefronts in America's so-called "culture war"?

The main factor causing the First Amendment's freedom of religion guarantees to become a flashpoint in American life has been the increasing secularization of our culture, accompanied by a concerted effort by influential segments of our society to trivialize religious convictions and to drive them to the margins of our culture. Stephen Carter's *The Culture of Disbelief,* subtitled *How American Law and Politics Trivialize Religious Devotion,* explains "some of the many ways in which our culture has come to belittle religious devotion, to humiliate believers, and even if indirectly, to discourage religion as a serious activity."[74] Carter argues persuasively that the cultural, political, educational, media, and even mainstream religious elites in America have been ever more effectively marginalizing religious beliefs and convictions as important, respected, or even legitimate factors in the nation's public policy arena.

The original title of Carter's book, before the publishers changed it, was *God as a Hobby.* Carter discusses this theme early in the book, describing how the dominant secular bias in our culture "holds not only that religious beliefs cannot serve as the basis of policy; they cannot even be debated in the forum of public dialogue. . . . Religion is like building model airplanes, just another hobby; something quiet, something trivial—and not really a fit activity for intelligent, public-spirited adults." Carter laments the increasingly antireligious bias in American jurisprudence and calls for religious convictions to be given their rightful and needed place in discussing the critical issues of our age, such as abortion, euthanasia, and capital punishment.

How has this secularization agenda impacted America and her institutions? One of the nation's most pervasive social institutions, the public schools, has provided the flashpoint for much of the public debate on religious expression in society. The Supreme Court, citing the need to implement their understanding of Jefferson's "wall of separation between church and state," began in the early 1960s to have a chilling effect on religious expression. The court's 1963 ruling that any state-sponsored activity related to the religious in the nation's public school must pass a "neutrality" test soon raised concerns that neutrality in theory devolved into hostility in practice. Indeed, that is precisely what happened, as subsequent judicial decisions, combined with widespread administrative misinterpretation by public school officials, produced not neutrality but a new religion of government-sponsored secularism.

By the 1990s, three decades of aggressive, secularizing neutrality hostile to religion had discriminated against the religious free exercise rights of students. Not only were schools, school officials, and teachers subjected to this hostility, but students' rights to freedoms of speech and assembly, not just a question of perceived violations of the First Amendment's establishment of religion clause, were restricted as well. Most Americans agreed that this secularizing of American society had gone too far. *Time* magazine ran a cover story entitled "One Nation Under God: Has the separation of Church and state gone too far?" and concluded:

For God to be kept out of the classroom or out of America's public debate by nervous school administrators or over-cautious politicians serves no one's interest. That restriction prevents people from drawing on the country's rich and diverse religious heritage for guidance, and it degrades the nation's moral discourse by placing a whole realm of theological reasoning out of bounds. The price of that sort of quarantine, at a time of moral dislocation, is—and has been—far too high. The courts need to find a better balance between separation and accommodation, and Americans need to respect the new religious freedom they would gain as a result.[75]

Multitudes of Americans, including many Southern Baptists, heartily agreed.

For the government to serve the common good of all citizens, religious and non-religious, we need to replace the posture of hostile neutrality with the constitutionally protected freedom *for* religion, not our current climate of freedom *from* religion. In the example of the public schools, this would look like religious pluralism, not secularism. This means respect and tolerance for the religious choices of others—whether they are Christian, Jewish, Muslim, Hindu, or unbelief. As long as the expression of that religious choice is student-accommodated, rather than school-sponsored, claims of "offense" would not override students' basic freedom exercise of that expression. We must accommodate *all* students' free exercise of their religious beliefs, while insisting there be no official sponsorship or favoritism of any particular religious perspective.

Imagine the richness of our American culture if enough people of faith awakened to the critical need of the hour and succeeded in turning the tide of our sterile, artificially secular public square that has segregated religion from the nation's public life. In an America under God's blessing, we would have an increased number of Christians freely exercising their right to express their beliefs in a manner that would incite tolerance if not approval of Christianity. But we would also have a posture of benevolent, accommodating neutrality supporting the free exercise of beliefs for all citizens of any and all religious persuasions, recognizing and protecting their rights to exercise their religious convictions in the public arena.

Commitment to the common good of all citizens must be built on the foundation of freedom for religion. The chilling effects of freedom *from* religion—that is, the posture of hostile neutrality—erodes the common good by undermining the moral values that have traditionally shaped American culture, illegitimately rejecting them as the intrusion of religion in public life.

What happens when moral values are torn down? We can see the effects clearly: moral chaos. When a society descends into moral chaos, it descends into social chaos as well. That places greater demand on families to instill moral values in its citizens. If the institution of the family is under attack as well, society is left vulnerable and unprotected.

Without strong families, you need a strong government. If the families are not providing the support system—that normal, developmental environment children need in order to grow up and become trustworthy and responsible adults—then government has to try to step in and provide that support system.

There's a reason why the Republicans are called the "Daddy Party" and the Democrats are called the "Mommy Party." The Daddy Party says, "You have to stand on your own two feet and take care of yourself; you shouldn't have to have other people taking care of you." The Mommy Party says, "We'll take care of you— we'll provide everything you need." People say there's a gender gap in the general population—women vote for the Democrats. *Unmarried* women do, but married women vote Republican: because those white males everyone wants to bash are their husbands. The gender gap is largely made up of single and divorced women who are looking to the government for what would normally be provided by a husband.

In Romans chapter 13, Paul explains that God designed the civil magistrate to punish evildoers and to reward those who do right. So we need a government that functions in that way. But if we don't have strong families, then we will need a strong government that limits liberty—or else we will have anarchy. I would prefer an America with very strong families, and very strong churches that are providing a support system for those in fractured families. An America blessed by God would have a clear balance of its three primary institutions: family, church, and government.

AN ECONOMY IN WHICH MONEY AND POWER ARE NOT THE SUPREME VALUES

The Bible has much to say about money and power, perhaps because our fallen natures leave us so liable to misuse them in destructive ways. The Old Testament speaks to economic issues that are with us today: inflation and the devaluing of currency (Haggai 1:6, Isaiah 1:22), credit difficulties (Proverbs 22:7; Psalm 37:21), lenders who take advantage of borrowers (Nehemiah 5:9–12), high taxes from big government (1 Samuel 8:11–18). In his parables, Jesus addressed interest rates (usury), profit and loss, wages, entrepreneurship, and contractual obligations.[76] The Bible clearly links obedience to God with economic well-being, and economic catastrophe with the failure of the people to live as God ordained.

Economic systems based on secular worldviews do not work, as socialism shows. However, unfettered capitalism—a free-market-only approach—doesn't work either. If we were operating under biblical principles, our economy would operate with a system of checks and balances similar to how the government operates. Human beings are sinful and selfish, so they're not going to work very hard unless they get to keep a very high percentage of what they make. We want to encourage productivity, but we also want to instill a sense of responsibility for stewardship of the wealth that is created.

Just as the government has the judicial branch, the executive branch, and the legislative branch, when the economy is operating for the common good it would have government controls for its judicial branch, to ensure a level playing field; business owners and economists for the executive branch, to make leadership decisions; and labor for the legislative branch to carry out and apply the decisions of the executive branch according to the controls established by the judicial branch.

If government has all the control, you have a Soviet-style command economy that won't work. If you have total control by capitalists, then you have the Robber Barons of the late nineteenth century, which doesn't work either. If you let the unions have complete control, the other segments are held hostage. You need to have all three—healthy and vibrant, functioning in their proper spheres—for the economy to work best and benefit the common life of the nation.

God never intended for us to be idle. Adam worked before the Fall, even in paradise. If we were living by God's ways instead of our own, people would be living longer, more productive lives because in older age they wouldn't be sitting around doing nothing waiting until they die. The old saying goes, "Use it or lose it." People might retire from their jobs, but they would continue to be active and productive, volunteering for mission trips, working as volunteers in hospitals, helping people take care of their elderly parents and grandparents at home. There would be fewer nursing homes because people would be healthier. More families would be stable and intact, caring for their loved ones at home, and they would have support networks through their local churches when the burdens of care were especially heavy.

We tend to discount the relationship between the health of the economy and the moral health of our culture, but the connections are clear. Dr. L. Gregory Jones, dean of Duke University Divinity School, wonders if the same quick-fix, short-term approach to parenting that keeps us from spending both quality and quantity time with our families is reflected in our get-rich-quick schemes in the economy—in particular, the popularity of state lottery games:

[Perhaps] the deeper problem with the lottery is that it encourages illusions of a personal quick fix to long-term economic issues. It is a commonplace that politics is inevitably preoccupied with the short term, but I wondered whether the lottery didn't corrode the long-term issues of forming worthy character. How do we begin to shape such virtues as prudence, honesty, courage and patience if we create illusions that anyone can—and perhaps will win the lottery?

Is this perhaps the logical extension of a dominant, amoral approach to economic and political life? Richard Sennett thinks so, and has written a polemical critique of "the new, flexible capitalism" and its impact on character. At the beginning of *The Corrosion of Character,* Sennett poses some powerful questions: "How do we decide what is of lasting value in ourselves in a society which is impatient, which focuses on the immediate moment? How can long-term goals be pursued in an economy devoted to the short term? How can mutual loyalties and commitments be sustained in institutions which are constantly breaking apart or continually being redesigned?"

Sennett's questions . . . point to the urgent need for the church to reclaim more focused attention on the long-term challenges of shaping character. If we want to bear witness to the gospel of forgiveness that offers new life, we must become skilled at cultivating patience, especially in a world that tries to make us ever more impatient.

But are we ready to take the long view? Can we really come to terms with a God who is patient, slow to anger, abounding in mercy and steadfast love? Are we willing to acknowledge that the making of disciples takes time? That perhaps one of the central reasons for the Bible's preoccupation with such issues as idolatry and greed has to do with the ways in which we search for fantasies to avoid the hard work of patiently shaping a holy character over time?[77]

The relationship between character and how we handle money is also highlighted by Crown Ministries, an organization devoted to teaching a Christian view of finances and practical ways of handling money. Founded by Christian businessman and finance author Howard Dayton, it later merged with Larry Burkett's Christian Financial Concepts to become Crown Financial Ministries, with the goal of reaching three hundred million people in fifteen years to help carry out the Great Commission. They issue a clear warning about the direction in which our country is moving:

Less money is being saved or contributed to churches and charitable organizations, and more is being spent on credit card interest, recreation, alcohol, gambling (primarily through state lotteries) and pets. *"For where your treasure is, there your heart will be also.... No one can serve two masters; for either he will hate the one and love the other, or he will be*

*devoted to one and despise the other. You cannot serve
God and wealth"* (Matthew 6:21–24).

Although this shift in spending focus has become
especially noticeable in the wake of America's economic slowdown, it is not a new trend. Rather, there
has been a steady and constant shift in spending
habits for the past two decades.

Many Christian leaders feel that this shift is
directly related to and can be traced back to the
decline of America's and the world's moral standards.

In fact, many feel that morality has such a direct
relationship to economic stability that when moral
character collapses the economic ramifications on a
nation can be devastating. The decline in moral standards and values not only affects our spiritual and
emotional welfare, it directly influences our value
system, priorities, consumer spending, charitable
contributions, personal debt, national debt, national
budget, government entitlement programs and how
they are funded, insurance, health care, our overall
economic well-being, and our ability to recover from
economic downturns.[78]

An America blessed by God would be morally and economically stable. But it would also be environmentally healthy,
because the Scriptures teach that we are stewards of natural
resources as well as material resources.

A VIEW OF THE ENVIRONMENT BASED ON STEWARDSHIP, NOT OWNERSHIP

Every day we are more aware, especially in the industrialized world, that land, sea, and air pollution caused by human ignorance and irresponsibility is endangering planet Earth. *Ecology* has been defined as "the study of the balance of living things in nature," but in the later decades of the twentieth century it was expanded to include what Francis Schaeffer described as "the destruction man had brought upon nature."[79]

When Schaeffer used that definition over thirty years ago, he was in a distinct minority among evangelical Christians in his sensitivity to environmental issues. Air pollution, toxic waste, tropical deforestation, depletion of the ozone layer, and the spate of local disputes over landfills have done much in the intervening three decades to focus the church's attention on the ecological crisis. More and more Christians are now aware that real, often critical, environmental problems exist, requiring serious, thoughtful responses. Both the problems and the concern they arouse have reached the stage in which something must and will be done in this, the first decade of the twenty-first century.

Evangelical Christians must decide whether we will engage the issue and aggressively join the debate or whether we will continue to leave the field to the margins of the Christian left and to a largely secular environmentalist movement which tends to devalue humanity as an aggressor species with no more right to the resources of the planet than any other form of life. The pantheistic and idolatrous tendencies exhibited by some elements of the environmentalist movement should concern Christians seriously.

In their efforts to create attitudes of value and worth for nature, "some modern thinkers have called for worshiping the natural order and they speak of that order in terms of a unity and purpose not allowing for an external creator," as Peter Hill pointed out in his article, "Biblical Principles Applied to a Natural Resources/ Environment Policy."[80] Similarly, Schaeffer observed, "The term 'God's creation' has no real place in pantheistic thinking. One simply does not have a *creation,* but only an extension of God's essence in which any such term as 'God's creation'—as though He were a personal God who created, whose creation was external to Himself (all of which is wrapped up in our Western phrase 'God's creation')—has no place."[81]

In fact, all people, Christian and non-Christian, should be deeply concerned about such pantheistic thinking because it allows for no really meaningful distinction between different aspects of creation, namely, human beings and other creatures. Consequently, pantheistic thinking lowers human beings rather than elevating the natural order. Whether the pantheistic thinking is "modern scientism that related everything back to the energy particle, or whether it is Eastern, and more religious and mystical in nature, eventually nature does not become high but man becomes *low.*"[82]

In the end, in the West, those who seek to argue for a special, unique place of value for human beings in creation are accused of anthropocentric, arrogant "speciesism"—defined as the artificial, erroneous, egocentric valuing of one's own species more highly than one ought. In Eastern pantheism (as in India), people allow cows and rats to consume food needed by human beings. Animals prosper while humans starve on the streets because no way exists to make a meaningful value judgment between a human being and a cow.

Many influential thinkers within the modern environmental movement not only espouse such views and beliefs which are antithetical to Judeo-Christian values but also believe Christianity deserves substantial blame for Western culture's often callous disregard and flagrant exploitation of nature and of the environment.

One of the most influential voices in this criticism of Christianity was Lynn White, Jr., a professor at UCLA. He published an extremely influential article in *Science* magazine entitled, "The Historical Roots of Our Ecological Crisis," in which he argued that although we live in a post-Christian age, we are still operating under the influence of Christian ideas. One of the most pernicious, he believed, was the Christian teaching that humanity transcended and dominated nature as a God-given trait and right. Therefore, White asserted, Christianity bore "a huge burden of guilt" for encouraging humanity's despoliation of nature.[83]

White explained that our view of ecology arises from our beliefs about who we are and how we are related to the world around us:

> Human ecology is deeply conditioned by beliefs
> about our nature and destiny—that is, by religion. . . .
> What we do about ecology depends on our ideas of
> the man-nature relationship. More science and more
> technology are not going to get us out of the present
> ecologic crisis until we find a new religion, or rethink
> our old one. . . . Both our present science and our
> present technology are so tinctured with orthodox

Christian arrogance toward nature that no solution
for our ecologic crisis can be expected from them
alone. Since the roots of our trouble are so largely
religious, the remedy must also be essentially religious. . . . We must rethink and refeel our nature
and destiny.[84]

White is absolutely right that the ecological issue has philosophical, religious, and ethical roots. As Francis Schaeffer commented on White's view, "Men *do* what they *think*. Whatever their
world view is, this is the thing which will spill over into the external world."[85]

What we think about who we are and what our relation is to
the Creator and His creation absolutely determines how we deal
with this issue, as well as how we deal with many others. The religious, the philosophical, and the ethical must be most important.
White and others who blame Christianity for the world's ecological plight have declared that not only do they want to redress how
the Judeo-Christian worldview has influenced our culture, but
they want to change the Judeo-Christian worldview itself.

The environmental critics of Christianity have misunderstood
and misapplied the message. Far too often what they have rejected
is not true Christianity but what Schaeffer called a "sub-Christian"
theory in a post-Christian era. This is in part because Christians
themselves have misunderstood or misapplied the message. Even
in the brightest moments of Christian history, such as the
Reformation epoch, Christianity has had its blind spots, as
Schaeffer pointed out: "At certain points the people in the stream
of the Reformation were inconsistent with the biblical teaching

they claimed to follow. Many areas existed in which people did not follow the Bible as they should have, but two are outstanding: first, a twisted view of race, and second, a noncompassionate use of accumulated wealth."[86]

I believe we should add a third major blind spot: a failure to adequately understand and bear witness to a truly biblical view of creation—of humanity's relation to it and to the God who created them both. What is a truly biblical view of the environment? We can summarize it in seven primary aspects of the Bible's teaching.

First, a biblical view begins with the Bible's opening declaration, in which God reveals that He is the Creator: "In the beginning God created the heavens and the earth" (Genesis 1:1).

Second, it continues with the revelation that His creation is valuable to Him apart from humanity, because He continually declared the creation "good" before He created human beings.

Third, God's care for His creation continued after the Fall. He told Noah that He was establishing a covenant "with you" and "with every living creature" (Genesis 9:8–17). Then He spoke of "a covenant between me and the earth." And the sign of that covenant was the rainbow. We should not allow God's rainbow to be commandeered and prostituted by the New Age and homosexual movements. It is a biblical and Christian symbol, and we ought to contend for it rather than to surrender it to our opponents.

Fourth, a biblical view of the environment affirms God's concern for and "valuing" of the creation in the fulfillment of His purposes for the redemption of all things. The apostle Paul makes clear that our redemption in Christ includes the creation: "The creation waits in eager expectation for the sons of God to be revealed. For the creation was subjected to frustration, not by its own choice, but by the will of the one who subjected it, in hope that the creation itself will be liberated from its bondage to decay and brought into the glorious freedom of the children of God" (Romans 8:19–21).

This does not mean that we will redeem the cosmos from the devastating effects of the Fall. It does mean that "cosmic regeneration" (*palingenesia*, Matthew 19:28) is part of Christ's ultimate redemption ministry.[87] The creation is important enough to God that God looks upon it as part of those things to be redeemed by the sacrifice, the death, the resurrection, the ascension, and the second advent of our Lord and Savior Jesus Christ.

Fifth, "the earth is the LORD's, and the fulness thereof" (Psalm 24:1 KJV). Yet we are also told that we are to have dominion (Hebrew *radah*, meaning "to rule") over the creation and to subdue it (Hebrew *kabash*, meaning "to bring into bondage," Genesis 1:26–28). These are strong, dominant words in the biblical text and leave no room for doubt that God has placed human beings first in creation. This human preeminence in the created order was extended when God told Noah, "Everything that lives and moves will be food for you. Just as I gave you the green plants, I now give you everything" (Genesis 9:3).

Sixth, God remains the Lord of creation even though He gives human beings authority for ruling over or superintending nature. He is the Lord of the earth. We are merely vicars and vice-regents—stewards.

Seventh, this strong teaching of human preeminence and dominion in the created order is balanced by God's announcement that He put human beings in the creation "to dress it and to keep it" (Genesis 2:15 KJV). The verb *dress* (*avadh*) means "to work, to till," and *keep* (*shamar*) means "to keep, guard, protect." Other passages detail God's expectations that human beings carefully manage land, wildlife, and domestic animals.[88]

The Bible is clear that creation belongs to God and we are stewards of His property, responsible for protecting His creation. We need to have reverence for human life, but we should have respect for all life. We don't have the right to treat a chicken the way we would treat a television set. A television set is a thing—a chicken is a living creature. God made a covenant with all of His creation—yes, a human being is more important than a chicken, but a chicken is more important than a television set.

We have the right to use animals and plants for human good, but we do not have the right to disregard living things or treat them as inanimate objects. We have the right to domesticate and raise cattle for human food, but we do not have the right to handle them in a callous, cruel, or cavalier manner. Just because we don't worship cows doesn't mean we have the right to abuse or mistreat them either. I don't eat veal because of the cruel way the calves are treated—I don't think we have a right to treat baby cows that way. We have the right to use animals when necessary for experimentation to find cures for things like polio and cancer, but we do not have the right to cause them unnecessary or undue pain. And we don't have the right, I believe, to cause pain and suffering to animals in order to perfect cosmetics as opposed to medicines.

Matthew Scully, former speechwriter for President George W. Bush and former editor of the *National Review,* stirred up controversy with his book *Dominion: The Power of Man, the Suffering of Animals, and the Call to Mercy.* He points out that human beings are prone to abusing power by forgetting that we are not the final authority:

> The people who run our industrial livestock farms, for example, have lost all regard for animals as such, as beings with needs, natures, and a humble dignity of their own. They treat these creatures like machines and "production units" of man's own making, instead of as living creatures made by God. And you will find a similar arrogance in every other kind of cruelty as well. . . . If I read my Bible right, then there is Good News even for the lowly animals—that love and mercy have come into the world, and we can be its agents. And when I think of the suffering of the creatures in our factory farms, laboratories, puppy mills, or of any animal neglected or mistreated by man, for me there is no more powerful question than to ask: "What would the Good Shepherd think of this?"[89]

The Scriptures tell us that as stewards of God's property, we are responsible to develop, but not to desecrate or dissipate, God's creation. We are required to develop God's creation and to bring forth its fruit and increase. Our Lord's parable of the talents underscores the Genesis admonition to "dress" the garden. The servant who buried his talent was severely reprimanded for his poor stewardship and lack of productivity with the talent entrusted to his care.[90]

The belief that God is the Creator and that He has created everything for a purpose has enormous significance and implications for the environmental issue. For Christians, seeking the perpetuation and viability of all the created order—until we can discern and discover what purpose God has for every living creature and plant—is a task of faith, stewardship, and enlightened self-interest.

A classic example is Madagascar's rosy periwinkle, which has been proven to have significant cancer-fighting properties. This benefit would have been lost to humankind if the plant had been eradicated before its anticancer potential had been discovered.

I am more firmly convinced than ever that we face an ecological crisis and that God holds us accountable for our stewardship of the creation and of its resources that He has entrusted to our care. That role of stewards, of course, extends to our children. I believe we have a responsibility to inform our young people of the problems and of the biblical principles that should inform our response. In doing so, we can further perform our duties as Christians and parents by inoculating our young people against the false, antibiblical teaching which so heavily suffuses much of the modern, secular environmentalist movement.

If we don't tell others what we believe and why we believe it on this issue, who will? If we do not practice what we preach, many of our young people, who are deeply concerned about this issue, will be carried to places that we would rather they not go and will draw conclusions that we would rather they not draw by exposure to false philosophies. These philosophies, for fallacious and antibiblical reasons, at least demonstrate concern about the creation.

We must help our young people and others by moving from principle to practice, from advice to application.

For those outside the Christian faith who have been environmentally involved, there is good new and bad news. The good news is that we can repent of past insensitivity and neglect. The bad news is that our advocacy for environmental concerns is based on a distinctly Christian worldview, which conflicts with their secular and often pantheistic views in many respects and will therefore yield solutions that might be at cross-purposes with their agenda. I pray that we will "be prepared to give an answer to everyone who asks" about our beliefs and behavior, in regard to both why we do what we do and "the hope" we have by the providence and grace of God (1 Peter 3:15).

The America that has been blessed by God will be far less polluted and far more environmentally friendly than the America of today. It will be an America that understands God's assignment to our ancestor when He put Adam in the garden to till it and maintain it. We tend the earth in order to bring forth its fruit, caring for the land on which we farm. When we cut down trees, we plant new ones. And we know that our caretaking responsibility is a lifetime assignment: retirement from salaried positions does not mean that we have license to amuse ourselves to death. We will still be productively involved in the care of creation.

It is certainly right and good to unstring your bow from having to labor for your bread by the sweat of your brow, but God never intended for any of us to be idle. Even before the Fall, Adam was put in the garden to till it and to keep it. It just became a lot more burdensome after the Fall because the creation was cursed with thorns and thistles. Therefore Adam had to work by the sweat of his brow to bring forth his living, and Eve had travail in childbirth.

The earth is the Lord's. That is the beginning of an environmental ethic. Its application extends beyond water supply and land use and air quality, to the deleterious effects on the environment of buying more cars and bigger houses than we need, and accumulating more "stuff" than we can use. It is a way of living out our Christian faith.

PROMOTING THE COMMON GOOD

After the death of Moses, God chose Joshua as his replacement to lead the Israelites across the Jordan River and take possession of the Promised Land. "As I was with Moses, so I will be with you," God told him. "I will never leave you or forsake you" (Joshua 1:5). Along with assurances of His constant presence, God gave Joshua counsel for successful leadership: "Do not let this Book of the Law depart from your mouth; meditate on it day and night, so that you may be careful to do everything written in it. Then you will be prosperous and successful" (Joshua 1:8).

To the degree that a nation's moral character conforms to God's moral law, it is bound to experience national well-being. But behavior alone does not bring lasting change; it must be built on the transformation of individual lives by the regenerating power of salvation in Jesus Christ.

Dallas Willard characterizes our American popular culture as so corrupt that darkness is no longer recognized as such. "[Moral] assuredness and self-righteousness in the practice of what, traditionally, would have been regarded as blatant evil is now the single most dominant feature of our common world. 'Sex and violence' in the media is but one symptom of this overwhelming fact and is very far from being the central issue. The central issue is the replacement of Jesus Christ as the light of the world by people like Nietzsche and John Lennon, or like Lenin and Mao."[91]

The answer, contends Willard, lies in the compelling reality of Christlike lives among people of faith. Cultural change will occur only when believers seek God in obedience and live out their faith as change agents:

> There is no effectual response to our current situation except for the children of light to *be* who and what they were called to be by Christ their head. Mere "reason" and "fact" cannot effectively respond, because they are now under the same sway of public spirit and institutions as are the arts and public life generally—and indeed as much of the "church visible" as well. Only when those who really do know that Jesus Christ is the light of the world take up their stand with him, and fulfill their calling from him to *be* children of light where they are, will there by any realistic hope of stemming the tide of evil and *showing* the way out of that tide for those who really want out.
>
> The call of Christ today is the same as it was when he left us here to serve him "even to the end of the age" (Matthew 28:20). We have not yet come to the "end of the age." That call is to be his apprentices, alive in the power of God, learning to do all he said to do, leading others into apprenticeship to him, and also teaching them how to do everything he said.
>
> If we follow *that* call today in our Christian groups, then, as in past times, the most important thing happening in our communities will be what is happening in our churches.[92]

· 11 ·

Imagine! Healing for our land . . .

A VISION FOR AMERICA

Some people see things the way they are and ask, "Why?" Others see things that never were and ask, "Why not?"

The difference between a dream and a vision is that a dream is something you wish were true. "Wouldn't it be wonderful if . . . ?" A vision is something you work to make true. "Imagine . . . it can happen here."

Life is uncertain, but there is one thing we know with absolute surety: Jesus Christ will come again. With the Lord, however, a day is like a thousand years, and a thousand years is like a day. We simply don't know when the Lord is coming back, so we need to follow His commands while we wait with expectation for His return.

Here is the entire law and commandments: *Love the Lord your God with all your heart and soul and mind, and love your neighbor as yourself* (see Matthew 22:37–39). This is no dream. It is a commandment. And it must become our vision of healing for America if we are to respond faithfully to God's invitation for the people who are called by His name to humble themselves, and pray, and seek His face, and turn from their wicked ways. Then He will hear and respond, and bring healing, and bless our country with an outpouring of blessing that can transform this country with a great reformation and revival of those who love others out of their great love for the Lord.

Yes, you need to become a change agent for Jesus Christ in your family, your church, your society. But it's not about you. It's about God and your neighbor. It's about serving God's purposes.

Unfortunately, what your culture has been telling you in multitudinous ways is that it is *all* about you. And no matter how well you think you have been resisting that message, all along you have been absorbing it through the pores of your skin. That's what culture does—it seeps into your consciousness. That's why my generation has a collective memory of the Cold War that my children can never have. They really can't understand what Ronald Reagan accomplished with the dismantling of the Berlin Wall, because they didn't live through the Cold War.

If you want to conjure up a feeling for the ethos of a particular time, you play music from that time. For some it would be the Beach Boys' "Good Vibrations," or, "We're in the dawning of the Age of Aquarius." Boomers have "Come on, baby, light my fire" reverberating in their memory tapes.

If you grew up in the United States of America—even if you went to evangelical churches, or a Catholic school, or you were raised in a home where you spent more time under your parents' influence than you did under the culture's influence through television, radio, movies, your peers, school—you have been immersed in the cultural message that *it's all about you*. It's about *your* self-fulfillment, self-gratification, self-improvement. The unholy trinity of American culture is "me, myself, and I."

This cultural message guarantees that there will be a correspondingly fruitless search for happiness, a fruitless search for peace, a fruitless search for fulfillment, a fruitless search for contentment. None of those is possible when you are constantly preoccupied with self. Former President William Jefferson Clinton, for good or ill, is a charismatic mirror of our nation. His autobiography—nearly a thousand pages long—has been on the bestseller lists so long it has probably set a record for a book of its length. What is it titled? *My Life*. That's a statement in and of itself.

"It's about *me, me, me, me, me*." That's the voice of our culture.

We know from the teaching of Christianity and the other great religions, and now also from hard scientific evidence, that we are not designed to live "me-only" lives. In other words, it's not good for man to be alone—big shock! In fact, we are hard-wired in three fundamental ways: first, to connect to other people—not just as a means of achieving self-fulfillment, but for the healthy growth of our physiology. We are designed to be in relational interaction with others.

We also know that, second, we are hard-wired to express our humanity in our masculinity and our femininity. It drives the politically correct crowd nuts when we get evidence yet again that men and women are different, because that implies that men and women need each other, that marriage is the unique union of two different genders.

Men are hard-wired to express their masculinity. They can either do it in brutish, self-centered ways, or they can do it in the self-sacrificing ways that have been shown so dramatically to us by those firemen and policemen who rushed into the Twin Towers on 9–11 and lost their lives saving others.

Women are hard-wired to express their humanity in their femininity. They can do it in the caricature of the shrinking violet or the manipulative shrew, or they can do it in nurturing, complementary ways from a quiet strength and inner beauty. God created us differently—not better or worse, superior or inferior, but different. So much so that even our brains operate differently in problem solving. That's just the way it works.

The third dimension of our hard-wiring is to connect to a purpose and a cause greater than ourselves—God. Researchers are now using the term *God* because it is so clear that we are made not for a knowledge of something transcendent, but for intimate participation in it—a relationship. So it's not about you; it's about finding God's purpose for your life in relation to others, in your identity as a man or woman, in your relation to Him.

The Bible says it, and science demonstrates it: the Good News is that you are a person of *significance*. Not because you say so, or because your mother says so, or because your social status says so, but because God created you that way. God never made a nobody. *Everybody* is a somebody to God.

There's more Good News: nobody can do as good a job of being the you that God created you to be, as you can! This is particularly important for teenagers to understand, because they spend so much time trying to be like somebody else. In fact, most of us adults spend so much time trying to be like somebody else! But nobody will ever be as good at being Jude Law as Jude Law is. No one could ever do as well at being Cary Grant as Cary Grant did. That's the way it is. But *nobody* can do as good a job of being me— the me that God created me to be—as I can, with God's help.

Every one of us is different. Do you have siblings? Are you different than they are (and aren't you grateful)? Even though you most likely have the same gene pool—the same mom and same dad—you're different. Why? Because God designed you and knitted you together in your mother's womb, as David exclaimed in Psalm 139. All of your parts were written in God's book before any of them came to be.

I'm grateful to my parents—my mother in particular—for raising me the way they did. When I was a young boy, I was gifted athletically, and my dad wanted me to grow up to be a professional baseball player. (Now please, understand this is not a knock on professional ballplayers.) "What do you think, Mom?" I asked. "Well, that's fine," my mother said, "but God made you for a more serious purpose."

God made *every one of us* for a serious purpose, and we need to find out what that serious purpose is. When we understand how God created us as unique individuals, then we can gladly be whoever He wants us to be—a welder, a loving husband, a child with ordinary achievements, a son or daughter who honors parents even when it is difficult to do so.

God calls some of us to become a loving, monogamous spouse—a person whose primary concern is for an intimate partner first, before his own needs. It is beautifully expressed in the phrase from the middle-English wedding covenant, "And with my body I thee worship." That certainly refers to the sexual dimension of marriage but not only that. It describes a posture of serving one's spouse, of seeking the fulfillment and happiness of the other. That is God's will for all of us who don't have the gift of celibacy.

It is also God's purpose for us to seek His will in every area of our lives, to become members of churches, knowing that God has promised everyone has at least one spiritual gift. God has given you at least one spiritual gift, and it is your responsibility and privilege to exercise it. Paul says in 1 Corinthians 12–13 that we're all members of the same body, and that God decides how the gifts are distributed, but everybody has at least one.

Are you a manager of a McDonald's? You have at least one spiritual gift. Are you a mom at home with small children? You have at least one spiritual gift. Are you a divorced person trying to rebuild a life from the dreams that are now in the past? You have at least one spiritual gift. If you are living your life in an honest, industrious way, carrying out your God-given calling as best you understand it, actively involved in your local church, and seeking to identify and develop the spiritual gift God gave you for ministering to your fellow Christians, then you are leading the life of purpose and significance that God created you to live and to perform.

Radical obedience doesn't mean high achievement, because radical obedience *is* the achievement. We're supposed to develop our talents so we can use them, but not just for our own selfish benefit. We may reap rewards, but everything we have is the Lord's. We're required to give back a tenth, but that is just the beginning, a way of acknowledging that all of it belongs to the

Lord; He just lets us have stewardship over that ninety percent. And we will give an account of that stewardship.

You can't know why you are the way you are until you know the Creator who created you. That happens only through a personal knowledge of Jesus Christ. Your purpose is to serve Him, to love Him, and to honor Him, and through that relationship to know who you are and why God put you here.

If you want to know who you are; if you want to know peace, love, joy, patience, and all the fruits of the Spirit; if you want to know what it means to be God's man in God's place in God's time, or God's woman in God's place in God's time, possibly with the partner God intended for you; doing what it is God has created you to do; then you need to get in the middle of God's will. God has told us how we can get in the middle of His will: through accepting Jesus Christ as our personal Savior and acknowledging Him as Lord (that means "Boss"), letting Him be on the throne of our lives.

When you seek God's face, He tells you who you are. That will impact every area of your life. It will impact who you are as a person. It will impact who you are as a spouse. It will impact who you are as a son or daughter, as a sibling, as a parent. It will impact who you are as a church member, and who you are as a citizen. When you allow the Lord to *be* the Lord in your life, then the Holy Spirit is able to create within you the fruit of the Spirit: *agape* love.

How do you love your neighbor as you love yourself? You don't. You allow the Holy Spirit to create that love within you. The vision for an America that God has blessed is a vision of an America that is full of God-blessed people. Jesus said that if you lose your life for His sake, you will find it. You will lose yourself in service to something larger than yourself: God's purpose for your life.

IS THE BEST YET TO BE?

There's no question that if the number of believers increased to reach a divine tipping point, we would see an America we have never seen before, a society that has not yet been created. Could that really happen? If it weren't possible, God wouldn't command us to live out radical obedience.

The apostle Paul tells us to adorn the doctrine of Christ in our lives,[93] in the same way that a woman adorns herself by wearing attractive jewelry or by fixing her hair in a particular way. If we live in radical obedience, we will make the doctrine of Christ more attractive.

Could the best be yet to be? Imagine it. There would be a huge shift in the media, because a lot more media people would be saved—spiritual men and women, able to understand spiritual things.

Single young men and single young women would be beating down the doors of churches to find spouses who will love them and serve them in the love and power of Christ.

Not everyone would be saved, but everyone would be impacted by the cultural norms, which would be primarily Judeo-Christian. People would be more likely to do the right thing because it would be the expected thing.

Are you thinking that this is a fantasy scenario?

First, dwell on this: God never calls us to do anything that He does not give us the ability to do.

Second, take your end-times views out of your mental pocket and put them on the table. Millennial views are not our business. No one knows the hour or the day of His coming, so let's just put all that speculation off to the side and leave it there. They are all opinions—and everybody has one. Everybody has a theory—I've got mine; chances are you've got yours. Let us make the main thing the *main* thing. And the main thing is that what God calls us to do, He empowers us to do as His children. And He is a keeper of His promises. So if enough of God's people—first of all, in our own individual lives—turn and repent and seek His ways, God will bless us as individuals, and He will bless our families. And if enough Americans are blessed as individuals, and enough Americans are blessed as families, then we will have churches that are blessed by God. And as the churches are blessed, our communities will be blessed, and ultimately the government will be blessed.

We have discussed what this would look like in the basic building block of society—the family. We know that being reared in single-parent homes is destructive to children. Something like 85 percent of men in prison were raised without dads.

New Orleans Seminary has a ministry in the Angola Prison that offers education courses. These guys are studying, learning, and getting diplomas. The ones who are in there for life are saved, trained, discipled, and called to preach, and they are ministering to their fellow prisoners. Guys are asking to be transferred from minimum security prisons to maximum security prisons so they can minister to the prisoners. The prison warden told our seminary president in New Orleans, "You know, this is an amazing thing. This is the first time anybody has ever said to any of these men, you are important. You have value. You have purpose."

We have no concept of how powerful that message is. If it can do so much in a prison population, then what would it do if *children* heard this message from their parents all the years they were growing up? Imagine if it were the norm, not the exception, for parents to affirm their children the way my mother affirmed me— "Richard, baseball is great entertainment, but God made you for a more serious purpose."

I don't mean that we should go back in time to a less turbulent era, such as the fifties. Were the fifties better for kids? Perhaps, more so than today. But it was better for boy kids than girl kids— at least in some ways. They weren't as likely to get raped or molested, you know. But we don't have to sacrifice one trade-off for another. I want us to imagine going to a place that has never been, where women are protected, where they are not raped and beaten every nine seconds as they are today. Where they are not sexually abused and dehumanized as sexual appliances and objects of pornography. But neither are they told they can't play competitive sports because it might injure their reproductive futures.

Clearly our vision is not for the fifties—although if we got what God intended, it might look a lot more like the fifties than it does today, but without the sexism and the racism. We would not see the unequal treatment of people of color. Neither would we see the unequal balance between men and women. I think it's only fair to say that in the 1950s men fell far short of loving their wives as Christ loved the church and gave himself for it. On the other side of the coin, it's fair to say that far too many fifties wives were very manipulative and far from respecting their husbands as unto the Lord.

Let us imagine a society in which the norm is stable homes—with husbands who love their wives and wives who love their husbands. With husbands who serve their wives and seek to always put their wives' needs above their own, and wives who respect their husbands. Where children are being reared in the nurture and the admonition of the Lord, and not provoked to wrath and anger. How different would our schools look? How different would our prisons look? They would be emptying so fast we would need a prison museum just to recall how it used to be. Would we still need prisons? Sure, but not nearly as many.

We probably wouldn't have the teacher shortage that we do now, either. We would have people who are teachers because God called them to be teachers. They wouldn't be opting out of teaching for higher-paying professions. Teachers would be paid more.

You could take almost every institution of our society and in a future of God's blessing, it would be radically different. What would best help to cure poverty in America? One single thing—if women married the fathers of their children. That alone would eliminate most of the poverty we have today, more than any other change in the United States, bar none.

Think about a society in which a significant portion, if not a majority, of the labor force worked as responsibly and as well as they could because they felt it was their moral obligation and responsibility. Productivity would rocket through the roof! We would have workers who were laboring to the best of their ability as unto the Lord, managers and bosses who were servant leaders, doing their best to be the kind of boss they would like to have. It takes a radical reorientation just to imagine it!

FINDING PURPOSE AND MEANING

You can bring the best that is yet to be into the present. Find out what God's purpose is for you, and follow it. "For it is by grace you have been saved, through faith—and this not from yourselves, it is the gift of God—not by works, so that no one can boast. For we are God's workmanship, created in Christ Jesus to do good works, which God prepared in advance for us to do" (Ephesians 2:8–10). That "prepared in advance" literally means "footprints." God has fore-ordained *an individual pathway of footprints* for you. He does not hand out off-the-rack wills for our lives. There are plenty of things in life we have in common, but God has an individual plan and an individual purpose for you that is perfectly suited to your individual, unique personhood.

It's not about you. It's about God's purpose for you, and for your life. It is in radical obedience to this purpose that you will find meaning in your life. It is where you will find purpose and meaning in your family. It is where you will find purpose and meaning in your church. It is where you will find purpose and meaning in your neighborhood, in your city, and in your country.

You will reflect what you spend time thinking about and with whom you spend time. What is the dream of most Americans? *The good life.* And how is the good life defined? *Freedom from financial worries.* What do most men want? *An endlessly satisfying sex life.* What do most women want? *A partner who provides security and emotional intimacy.*

Take a look at television, and you will see the vision of most Americans for the good life. "If I could just have a million dollars." "If I could just find the right partner who will meet all my needs."

"If I could just satisfy these desires and urges for what I want out of life." Talk about a pagan, self-idolizing vision—to be free to satisfy whatever urge or desire you have! Even God took off only one day out of the week. And before the Fall, Adam worked in the garden. It got tougher after the Fall, because the ground was cursed. But in paradise, he was to till the garden and keep it. He wasn't just sitting there contemplating his navel. He had tasks, responsibilities, and obligations.

God did not create us as idle, self-indulgent creatures. But that's the image most Americans have of the good life. There's nothing like sudden wealth to reveal the real person. You give most Americans all the money they ever needed, and you would see very interesting changes in behavior. But we know that this dream will never bring happiness and contentment. It will never yield a sense of purpose and meaning. All the money in the world doesn't keep marriages from breaking up—in fact, it usually makes the divorces even nastier.

Dr. W. A. Criswell, a mighty preacher and former president of the Southern Baptist Convention, used to tell about a fellow who was living in Oklahoma when they were discovering oil on everybody's land. Twenty straight farms struck oil, but for some reason when they got to this fellow's property line, the oil stopped. He told his pastor that he couldn't understand why God allowed it to happen this way. But when he looked back on it as an older man, he saw the chain of consequences that had happened to the twenty other families. "You know, Pastor," he said, "for every one of those families it's led to divorce. It's led to spoiled children who have gone off in self-indulgent fashion. I've learned to be grateful that God spared me that temptation."

Money is not the root of all evil—it's the love of money. It's our attitude toward money. We keep trying to nourish our spiritual and emotional needs with material wealth, and we're dying of spiritual and emotional starvation.

The contrast could not be more stark between "it's about you" versus "it's not about you." We are not our own gods. We find purpose and meaning in life only in finding out who we are in God's design and for God's purposes. Our greatest blessings will come through finding God, serving God, and becoming who God created us to be.

WILL IT START WITH YOU?

It's not about you—but it may depend on you. It may begin with you. You may never know whose life will be transformed by your radical obedience.

Dr. Tony Evans is the senior pastor of Oak Cliff Bible Fellowship Church in Dallas (five thousand members) and president of The Urban Alternative, a ministry devoted to bringing about change in urban communities through the church. His radio broadcast is heard across the nation and around the world. His speaking ministry has included Promise Keepers, crusades, and Bible conferences. He is chaplain for the Dallas Mavericks and past chaplain for the Dallas Cowboys. He has written over seventeen books, including one entitled *The Best Is Yet to Come.*

Tony Evans's father, an African-American, got saved through the witness of a fellow worker, a white man who told him about Jesus. He went home and told his wife about his conversion, but his wife just laughed at him. "That's just foolish nonsense," she said, and she continued to chew him out, be disrespectful, and criticize him. Every night, Tony says, he could hear his dad alone downstairs, praying for his wife and family. Finally, one night he heard his mother jump out of bed and run down the stairs. "I don't understand this," she said to him, "but whatever it is you have, I want it." That led to her being saved, and to Tony and his brother being saved.

Are you ever tempted to become cynical or lose heart when you do not see immediate results of God's redeeming work? "This is a pipe dream after all," you might say in such moments. "Things are getting worse every day. I pick up the newspaper and can't help but think, 'That's such a wonderful message that Dr. Land has, but it's not realistic.'" When such times come, remember that *it is not about you*. It is about what God is doing, and sometimes that remains hidden to our eyes. Turn your focus away from what you do *not* see, and focus on "Whatever is true, whatever is noble, whatever is right, whatever is pure, whatever is lovely, whatever is admirable—if anything is excellent or praiseworthy—think about such things" (Philippians 4:8).

Elisabeth Elliot's life as a missionary to Indians in South America became international news when in 1956 her husband, Jim Elliot, and four other missionary men were murdered by Auca Indians in Ecuador. Elisabeth has written about this tragic event and its redemptive aftermath in several books. She has also written a biography of missionary and prolific writer Amy Carmichael, her spiritual mentor, who battled her own tragedies in pioneering a rescue work among India's children. Reflecting on much of the hidden work of Amy Carmichael's life, Elliot writes:

Our enemy and God's is always busily at work distorting our vision, throwing confusion into our minds lest we see the glory that God is waiting to show us in everything that makes up our lives—the people we love, our homes, our work, our sufferings. Deep things he makes us believe are shallow, high things low, our deep hunger for the transcendent a will-o-the-wisp. Look for proofs, he whispers. Where are the proofs? Let's have statistics. Did it work? . . . Is it true? The questions are valid ones. They cannot be ignored, nor can they be answered finally except in the realm where faith operates, the Unseen. We may and we must look at the visible, but let us remember that there is far more to be taken into account. We may not always insist on visible corroborations, for they don't tell the whole story. The gold, silver, and precious stones may be in safe deposit where we can't get at them.[94]

You may never know the impact your radical obedience might have on someone else's life. It might be the birth of a new faith, or the reawakening of a deadened faith.

It might be the mending of a broken life.

It might be the renewal of purpose in a purposeless life.

A poem that has been very important to me in the past, and continues to have a tremendous impact on my life, is Robert Frost's "Stopping by Woods on a Snowy Evening." While I was a student at Princeton University, I kept a handwritten copy of this verse taped to the headboard of my bed so I would see it every morning:

> The woods are lovely, dark and deep,
> But I have promises to keep
> And miles to go before I sleep,
> And miles to go before I sleep.

"I have promises to keep, and miles to go before I sleep"—that is about purpose, obligation, and responsibility. It's not about sitting around looking at the woods on a snowy evening. This doesn't mean that you don't sometimes unstring your bow. There has to be balance in every life. But it's not about you and your personal enjoyment or pleasurable distractions.

You are not your own; you have been bought with a price. That's what Paul said to the Corinthian Christians (1 Corinthians 7:23). You have been ransomed from the slave market, saved to serve. Your promise to keep is to fulfill God's purpose.

God is the one who created you. God owns you. You belong to God. He created you to love Him and serve Him, to love your neighbor and serve your neighbor. You will find your purpose and meaning in service to God, in service to others through God.

Who is your neighbor? *Everybody.* If Christians are by their behavior and actions giving a better witness to the gospel, it certainly means that some of the unsaved will be saved. They will see their good works and say, "There is a God after all."

The early church took the worst hostility that the Roman Empire could throw at it and overcame it. Ultimately, slavery in the Roman Empire was ended. Before the church's influence, commonplace social mores included abortion, infanticide, child sacrifice, and slavery. After the church, those practices came to an end. Did everybody get saved? No. Did Judeo-Christian values become the norm in that society? To a significant degree, yes.

Early believers thought that Christ was going to return quite soon, but they did not retreat to eschatological ghettos. They confronted the Roman Empire at every instance with the transforming gospel of Jesus Christ.

If a journey of a thousand miles begins with a single step, then the transformation of a culture and a society begins with a single life changed.

Imagine: the spiritual transformation of a nation begins with the spiritual transformation of one life.

What is God accomplishing in your life? Where are you with the Lord? The spiritual blessings poured out on America will begin with the spiritual changes in a single life.

Could it be yours? Should it be yours?

Amen. God bless you, and God bless America.

ENDNOTES

1. Lyrics to this song are posted in many places: for example, on www.john-lennon.com.

2. From "Amnesty Imagine and Human Rights Interview with Yoko Ono, posted on www.amnestyusa.org/imagine/world_stage/yoko_ono.html.

3. Isabel Garcia-Zarza, "Castro Hails Once-Shunned Lennon as Fellow Dreamer," Reuters News Service, 8 December 2000, 7:42 p.m. ET.

4. "Matters of Faith: Religion in Public Life: The Ninety-Sixth American Assembly, 23–26 March 2000, Arden House, Harriman, New York (a public document distributed by The American Assembly, Columbia University, 475 Riverside Drive, Suite 456, New York, NY 10115). The American Assembly was established by Dwight D. Eisenhower at Columbia University in 1950. It holds nonpartisan meetings and publishes authoritative books to illuminate United States policy.

5. Richard D. Land, *Real Homeland Security: The America God will Bless* (Nashville: Broadman & Holman, 2004).

6. Brian Gonsalves and Ken A. Paller, "Neural events that underlie remembering something that never happened," *Nature Neuroscience* (December 2000), vol. 3, no. 12, 1316–321.

7. Andy Stanley, *Visioneering* (Sisters, Oreg.: Multnomah, 1999), 17–18.

8. Paraphrased from Habakkuk 3:2.

9. I am paraphrasing Gideon's story from Judges chapter 6. Quotation marks indicate direct quotes from the NIV.

10. Malcolm Gladwell, *The Tipping Point: How Little Things Can Make a Big Difference* (New York: Little, Brown, 2000; paperback Back Bay Books, 2002).

11. Joel Belz, "Downsizing," *World* (3/10 July 2004), 6.

12. Belz, "Downsizing," 6.

13. Boris Pasternak, from "After the Storm" (1958), in *Poems of Boris Pasternak,* trans. Lydia Pasternak Slater (New York: Routledge, 1984), n.p.

14. Peter Singer, *Animal Liberation* (New York: Ecco Press, 2001).

15. From the mission statement of the American Civil Liberties Union.

16. Peter Singer, "A Philosophical Self-Portrait," in *The Penguin Dictionary of Philosophy* (London: Penguin UK, 1997), 521-22.

17. Peter Singer, *Rethinking Life and Death* (New York: St. Martin's Press, 1995), 197–98.

18. In a telephone call to the March for Life participants, 22 January 2004.

19. *The Baptist Faith and Message* (Nashville: Southern Baptist Convention/LifeWay Christian Resources, 2000), 10.

20. Charles Krauthammer, "Why Lines Must Be Drawn: Stem cells present a complex moral issue. Shame on Democrats for polarizing it," *Time* (23 August 2004), 78.

21. Rick Warren, *The Purpose-Driven Life: What on Earth Am I Here For?* (Grand Rapids: Zondervan, 2002).

22. Nancy R. Nangeroni, "Transgenderism: Transgressing Gender Norms," for the International Foundation for Gender Education, posted online at www.gendertalk.com/tgism/tgism.shtml.

23. *Baptist Faith and Message*, 10.

24. Quoted by Jeffrey Hodgson in "Guevara, Kinsey Revolutionize Toronto Film Fest," *Variety*, 13 September 2004, 07:03 ET, www.reuters.com/newsArticle.jhtml?type=topNews&storyID=6224435.

25. Hodgson, "Guevara, Kinsey Revolutionize Toronto Film Fest."

26. From the brochure "A Woman's Guide to Sexuality," published by *Planned Parenthood* (PPFA Web site © 1998–2004 Planned Parenthood® Federation of America), www.plannedparenthood.org/WOMENSHEALTH/sexuality.htm.

27. "A Woman's Guide to Sexuality," *Planned Parenthood*.

28. The Alan Guttmacher Institute (AGI), *In Their Own Right: Addressing the Sexual and Reproductive Health Needs of American Men* (New York, AGI, 2002); AGI, unpublished tabulations of the 1995 National Survey of Adolescent Males; and AGI, unpublished tabulations of the 1995 National Survey of Family Growth.

29. AGI, *Sex and American Teenagers* (New York, AGI, 1994).

30. AGI, "Why Is Teenage Pregnancy Declining? The Roles of Abstinence, Sexual Activity and Contraceptive Use" (New York, AGI, 1999).

31. AGI, "Teenage Sexual and Reproductive Behavior in Developed Countries: Can More Progress Be Made?" (New York, AGI, 2001).

32. Ibid.

33. Jessica R. Cattelino and Brenda J. Marston, "From Sexologists to Sexual Liberation: Books in the Human Sexuality Collection, 1880–1973," http://rmc.library.cornell.edu/HSC/fly/pre1973nonfiction.htm#nt1.

34. *Final Report of the Attorney General's Commission on Pornography* (Nashville: Rutledge Hill, 1986), 3.

35. Final Report of the Attorney General's Commission on Pornography, 486.

36. From the author's recollections based on notes during the meeting, November 12, 2002.

37. Linda J. Waite, Don Browning, William J. Doherty, Maggie Gallagher, Ye Luo, and Scott M. Stanley, "Does Divorce Make People Happy? Findings from a Study of Unhappy Marriages," published by the Institute for American Values (1841 Broadway, Suite 211, New York, NY 10023). This study is available online from the institute's Web site, www.americanvalues.org.

38. Barbara Dafoe Whitehead and David Popenoe, "The State of Our Unions: the Social Health of Marriage in America," published by The National Marriage Project. Downloaded 25 July 2002 from http://marriage.rutgers.edu/TEXTSOOU2002.htm.

39. Charles Colson, "For Better or Worse . . . Mostly Worse," BreakPoint Online (24 July 2002), downloaded 25 July 2002, http://www.breakpoint.org/Breakpoint/ChannelRoot/FeaturesGroup /BreakPointCommentaries.

40. From a Census 2000 Brief, "Employment Status: 2000," by Sandra Luckett Clark and Mal Weismantle, released August 2003 in "United States Census 2000," U.S. Census Bureau (U.S. Department of Commerce: Economics and Statistics Administration).

41. Figures cited in this chapter and not otherwise documented are drawn from the study "Why Marriage Matters: Twenty-One Conclusions from the Social Sciences," cosponsored by Center of the American Experiment; Coalition for Marriage, Family, and Couples Education; and The Institute for American Values (New York: Institute for American Values, 2002), available on the Internet at http://www.marriagemovement.org/Why MarriageMatters.html.

42. K. J. S. Anand, and P. R. Hickey, "Pain and Its Effects in the Human Neonate and Fetus," *New England Journal of Medicine* (19 November 1987), vol. 317, no. 21, 1321–329; available online at www.cirp.org/library/pain/anand/.

43. "Expert Report of Kanwaljeet S. Anand, M.B.B.S., D.Phil." to the Northern District of the U.S. District Court in California, 15 January 2004.

44. "National Fact Sheet 2002," CWLA, available online at http://www.cwla.org/advocacy/nationalfactsheet02.htm. Figures cited apply primarily to the years 1999 and 2000.

45. "The Foundation for Child Development Index of Child Well-Being, 1975–2002, with Projections for 2003: A Composite Index of Trends in the Well-Being of Our Nation's Children" (Durham, N.C.: Duke University, 2004). Research was conducted by The Brookings Institution, in cooperation with the Child Welfare Forum and Duke University. This study is available online at http://www.brookings.edu/dybdocroot/comm/events/20040324index.pdf.

46. Deborah A. Dawson, "Family Structure and Children's Health and Well-Being: Data from the 1988 National Heath Interview Survey on Child Health," *Journal of Marriage and the Family,* 1991, 53:573–584.

47. Sara McLanahan and Gary Sandefur, *Growing Up with a Single Parent: What Hurts, What Helps* (Cambridge, Mass.: Harvard University Press, 1994), xii.

48. Ed Young, *The Ten Commandments of Marriage: The Do's and Don'ts for a Lifelong Covenant* (Chicago: Moody, 2003).

49. Quoted from a live interview conducted by the author in Nashville, Tennessee, 9 March 2004. Used by permission.

50. Adapted from *Hardwired to Connect: The New Scientific Case for Authoritative Communities,* a Report to the Nation from the Commission on Children at Risk, sponsored by YMCA of the USA, Dartmouth Medical School, and the Institute for American Values (New York: Institute for American Values, 2003).

51. Ed Young, *Kid CEO: How to Keep Your Children from Running Your Life* (Nashville: Warner Faith, 2004), 4–5.

52. *Final Report of the Attorney General's Commission on Pornography,* xxxvii.

53. Ibid., 486.

54. Ibid., 486.

55. Ibid., 492.

56. From an interview conducted with Dr. Ed Young by the author on the *For Faith & Family* radio show, broadcast 9 March 2004.

57. Peg Tyre, Julie Scelfo, and Barbara Kantrowitz, "The Power of No," *Newsweek* (13 September 2004), vol. CXLIV, no. 11, 46.

58. Ibid., 44.

59. Ibid., 46.

60. Ibid., 48.

61. Ibid., 46–47.

62. Ibid., 47.

63. Ibid., 48.

64. Ibid., 45.

65. Ibid., 48.

66. Young, *Kid CEO,* 8–9.

67. See Genesis 12:10–20, in which Abraham ("Abram" at this point) insists that Sarai (later "Sarah") lie to the Pharaoh that she is Abram's sister. He knew that the Egyptian ruler would want Sarai for his harem—and would first kill her husband before taking Sarai as a royal concubine.

68. See Exodus 2:11–14.

69. See 2 Samuel chapter 11.

70. Dallas Willard, *Renovation of the Heart* (Colorado Springs, Colo.: NavPress, 2002), 224.

71. Laurie Winer, "Bening on Bening," *More* (November 2004), 86.

72. Ibid., 87.

73. Jason Byassee, "A cure for what ails us," *Christian Century* (2 November 2004), 35.

74. Richard D. Land, *Critical Issues: A Baptist's View of Prayer in Schools* (Nashville: Christian Life Commission of the Southern Baptist Convention, 1996), 2.

75. *Time,* 9 December 1991.

76. See the parables of the pounds (Luke 19:12–26), the talents (Matthew 25:14–30), and the workers in the vineyard (Matthew 20:1–16).

77. L. Gregory Jones, "Faith Matters," *Christian Century* (11 April 2001), 3.

78. "Morality and Economics," Crown Financial Ministries, posted online at www.cfcministry.org/library/articleview.asp?op=1736sjh&id=7510837.

79. Francis Schaeffer, *The Complete Works of Francis A. Shaeffer, a Christian World View,* 6 vols. (Westchester, Ill.: Crossway, 1982), 5:4 from *Pollution and the Death of Man: The Christian View of Ecology* (1970).

80. Peter J. Hill, "Biblical Principles Applied to a Natural Resources/Environment Policy," *Christians in the Marketplace Series,* vol. 4, *Biblical Principles and Public Policy,* ed. Richard C. Chewning (Colorado Springs: NavPress, 1990), 170.

81. Schaeffer, *Complete Works,* 5:14–15.

82. Ibid., emphasis added.

83. Lynn White Jr., "The Historical Roots of Our Ecological Crisis," in Schaeffer, *Works,* 5:63.

84. White Jr., "Ecological Crisis," 63, 67–69.

85. Schaeffer, *Complete Works,* 5:6.

86. Ibid., 141.

87. As explained in *Criswell Study Bible,* ed. W. A. Criswell (Nashville: Thomas Nelson, 1979), 113n.

88. See Leviticus 25:1–5, Deuteronomy 22:6, and Deuteronomy 25:4.

89. "Exploring Dominion," a Q&A by Kathryn Jean Lopez, *National Review Online* (3 December 2002), posted online at http://www.nationalreview.com/interrogatory/interrogatory 120602.asp.

90. See Matthew 25:14–30.

91. Willard, *Renovation of the Heart,* 231.

92. Ibid., 231–32.

93. See Titus 2:10 KJV.

94. Elisabeth Elliot, *A Chance to Die: The Life and Legacy of Amy Carmichael* (Old Tappan, N.J.: Fleming H. Revell, 1987), 377–78.

SCRIPTURE INDEX

NAME AND
SUBJECT INDEX